COACHING JOBSEEKERS

Karin Tenelius

www.tuffledarskapstraning.se

All rights reserved
Copyright©Tuff Ledarskapsträning AB, 2010
Translation by Alexandra Simpson
Cover photo/idea by Birgitta Wahlberg
Photo of the author by Anders J Larsson
Edited by Språkligheter, Eva Rozgoni
Graphic design and illustrations by Heidi Sundström
Printed by Tallinna Raamatutrükikoja OÜ, Estonia, 2010
ISBN 978-91-978873-1-1

CONTENTS

Foreword 7

COACHING JOBSEEKERS – INTRODUCTION
The hard facts of jobb hunting 10
Background 11
My personal outlook and philosophy 13
The value of coaching jobseekers 15
Aim of the book 17
Contents 19
Some common challenges when coaching jobseekers 20

SECTION 1 – COACHING AS A WAY OF 'BEING' RATHER THAN 'DOING'
What exactly is coaching all about? 22
Good coaching is a product of who you are 24
Five attitudes of a good coach 25
    Relating to people´s potential 25
    Understanding the limits of your responsibility 28
    Clarifying and summarising 32
    Accepting the situation as it is 33
    Not having your own agenda 35
Developing a coaching approach – integrating the five attitudes 37

SECTION 2 – TRADITIONAL ISSUE-BASED COACHING
Coaching that deals with issues compared with attitude 40
Basic coaching skills 41
    Listening 41
    Asking questions 44
    Having empathy 50
Their goal is your assignment 52
Traps in issue-based coaching 53
Developing your basic skills 55
    Listening skills 55
    Questioning skills 56

SECTION 3 – THE BASIC PRECONDITIONS FOR COACHING
Create the preconditions for coaching 60
    Clarify the value of job coaching 61
    Deal with lack of confidence 62
    Clarify the purpose of the coaching and what it involves 63
    Clarify that the aim is to find work 65
    Confirm willingness to be coached 66
    Ensure the dialogue is comfortable 67
Health problems and overarching personal problems 68
    Ill health 68
    Overarching personal problems 69
    Rehabilitation 70

Concluding words about creating conditions conducive to coaching 71

SECTION 4 – ATTITUDE-BASED COACHING
Focus on unproductive attitudes 74
Listen at new levels 77
    Listen for who the person is 78
    Listen for the underlying intention 79
Frank and honest feedback 81
    A structure for feedback 83
Traps in attitude-based coaching 87
Developing skills in attitude-based coaching 89

SECTION 5 – SOME COMMON CHALLENGES
Mixed roles – coach and government employee 92
Specific goals 95
About results, effectiveness, and when we get stuck 96
    Being stuck 97
Common unproductive attitudes 100
    "It's impossible to get a job" 100
    "I can't/don't want to choose …" 104
    "I'm not good enough" 105
    "But I'm 57 …" and other barriers 107

SECTION 6 – SOME TOOLS
Tools for managing a job search 112
    Your purpose in life is your starting-point 112
    Being specific and selective 114
    Job structure 116
    The job application 118
    Networks 118
    Backward planning 119
    Before the interview 121

SECTION 7 – SOME ILLUSTRATIVE EXAMPLES
Coaching in practice – real cases 126
    Changed her attitude to the barriers 126
    Took a stand for the value of her own contribution 126
    From impossible to considering it possible 127
    Financial problems got in the way 127
    Found his own answer 128
    From second best to living her dream 128
    New way of looking at his skills 129
    Victim of circumstances takes responsibility for the real barriers 130
    From dependent to independent 130
    From focusing on barriers to focusing on strengths 131
    His dream was within reach 131
    'Safe' searching is not always successful 132

SECTION 8 – COACHING GROUPS
Laying the groundwork for coaching in groups 134
What you need to talk about 136
    Relationship to the activities and groundrules for the group 136
    Mistrust and scepticism 136
    What's in it for me? 138
    What do I need a coach for? 139
    Choosing to participate 140
    Going from consumer to activist 141
    Who is responsible for getting the job? 142
    Can I consider it possible? 143
    Will we change the circumstances or get a job? 144
    The communication contract 144
Traps when coaching groups 145
Concluding words about group coaching 146

SECTION 9 – TRAINING SUPPORT
Support to help you get started 150
    Commitment 150
    Reminders 150
    Part of your daily life 150
    Traps are the key to your future skills 151
    Plan your training 151
    Make sure you get feedback 151
Confront traps 152
All the exercises in the book 154

SECTION 10 – AND FINALLY
Responding to the challenges 160
    How do I motivate a person who has given up hope? 160
    How do I coach spoilt young people who don't want to do anything at all? 160
    What do I do about someone who hides behind their health issues,
    even when they have not been signed off sick? 160
    How do I get people over 55 to want to have a job? 161
    What do you do about someone who doesn't understand that they are too choosy? 161
    How do you get a person to relocate in order to get a job? 161
    What do you do when even you think a person is a hopeless case? 161
Common questions 162
    Isn't this a form of therapy? 162
    Isn't coaching enormously time-consuming? 162
    How long does it take to train to be a jobseeker coach? 162

Some uncomfortable truths about jobseeker coaching 163

Concluding words 164

Acknowledgements 165

FOREWORD

People have much greater potential than they actually use.
 People are responsible for finding a job themselves.
 People can cope with constructive criticism even though it may hurt. The fact is it will make them even stronger.

These are some of the points of departure for Karin Tenelius in her book on coaching jobseekers. For me, this seems to be the right approach. That these points even need to be stated highlights the current crisis in unemployment.

The spread of the victim mentality amongst many jobseekers (with the help of the government) needs to be stopped. A perception has crept in that it is alright to feel sorry for unemployed people (and for yourself if you are unemployed), that it is alright for jobseekers to give up and expect the government to fix them up with a job, that it is fine to live on state benefits indefinitely. It seems to be accepted that the state can throw taxpayers' money at ineffective initiatives and sink resources into a system that needs to be overhauled from the bottom up. In a way, being unemployed has become equated with being helpless, and this thinking has permeated our society.

It is time to change our approach. Being successful in finding a job is less about going on courses and more about the jobseeker's attitude and outlook, as Karin Tenelius quite rightly stresses in her book. It is about changing what nowadays is often a passive approach to unemployment to one where the jobseeker takes responsibility for their situation and taps into their own potential. Tricky, in the opinion of many (myself included). Simple, says Karin. You can change your frame of mind quickly, she writes, if you just want to.

And that is where the coach's efforts should be directed, at empowering the jobseeker to find their own solution to their situation, because nobody else can do it for them.

It may not be easy, but what Karin Tenelius describes is basically straightforward. Clearly it is not for the coach to find a job for the jobseeker. Rather, it is the coach's task to stimulate the desire and ability in the jobseeker to go out and do it for themselves. Coaching is about unleashing the inner strength of another person so that they are able themselves to achieve the results they want, writes Karin. It is a matter of listening and asking questions, something we could all do with being better at.

Karin also writes that coaching is about connecting with people's potential, not their shortcomings. It also involves having the courage to talk frankly, because no jobless person feels better for being mollycoddled. On the contrary, tough but constructive criticism can work miracles.

In this book, Karin Tenelius presents plenty of challenges. To effectively coach a jobseeker often means you must first tackle your own preconceptions and ambitions. There are lots of pitfalls on the path to becoming an effective coach, and this book offers some tough exercises in self-awareness for those coaches who are ready and willing to increase their own effectiveness.

Perhaps one of the most important pieces of advice from Karin Tenelius is that one's ultimate goal in life should be the starting-point when looking for a job. To build your career around what you are really passionate about is the only sustainable starting-point in the long term. It also means increased commitment to the process, and consequently enhances the end result. Those who say that jobseekers can't afford the luxury of searching for a job they really care about are fundamentally wrong. Narrow your search but go about it in the right way, is Karin's view.

For the coach who wants to help take us from a society where jobseekers are found work by someone else to one where they are encouraged to realise their own potential, Karin Tenelius' book is a must.

Mia Odabas, business journalist and moderator

COACHING JOBSEEKERS
– INTRODUCTION

THE HARD FACTS OF JOB HUNTING

Nobody, not even a government Job Centre employee, can find a sustainable long-term job for you.

Finding a job depends entirely on your attitude.

An unproductive attitude is guaranteed to keep you unemployed, regardless of the situation in the job market.

Being convinced that it is impossible to get a job means you won't get one.

If you cannot answer "yes" to the question "Would you hire yourself?", you are not going to get a job.

It can take some time to find a job, but getting a job does not depend on how much time you spend looking – it is about what you do and how you go about it.

BACKGROUND

During the economic downturn of the early 90's, people who had been made redundant and were seeking work were streaming onto the job market. At that time in Sweden the recruitment industry was virtually non-existent and the Government Employment Office couldn't cope with the huge numbers of people registering for work.

I was working at that time as a training consultant, mainly in the service industry and marketing field. Like many other consultants I was often asked to undertake assignments connected to the jobseeker activities created by various agencies. This turned out to be where my mission lay. I had already become aware of the concept of coaching through American career consultants and training agencies, but it was not something that had been used in Sweden up to that point.

In those years, I met many thousands of people in various support programmes for jobseekers. Some courses lasted as long as 16 weeks, others were shorter and more targeted. I met academics and business people, as well as those with fewer qualifications and from less skilled professions. I met young people and older people, new Swedish citizens, people from the far northern and southern regions of Sweden and those from the main cities of Stockholm and Gothenburg. During those years, the whole of Sweden became my field of operation.

After a while I came to an important realisation. The decisive factor in whether people found work or not *had almost nothing to do with their qualifications*: whether they got a result depended on *their outlook, their mindset, their attitude*. This observation made me start approaching my work in a whole different way. Instead of discussing job applications, how to write a CV, interview techniques and so on, I developed a dialogue with people around their attitude to looking for work. These interactions were aimed at giving people the opportunity to change their outlook from an unproductive to a productive one. This proved to be a highly effective coaching method for supporting people in their job search.

The period of high unemployment ended almost overnight and there was no longer a demand for the support and coaching of jobseekers. At that point I directed my energies at the fields of trade and industry. I discovered there that my approach and methods involved in shifting unhelpful thought patterns were equally applicable to the area of leadership, and with extremely positive results. But that is a whole different story.

After a few years of economic boom, the bubble burst, and once again unemployed people poured onto the job market. This time, however, there were both unemployment programmes and careers advice services in place, available from both the private and public sectors. Coaching for jobseekers became a sought-after skill, and I was engaged by many agencies in the recruitment industry and trained hundreds of coaches in my method. At about the same time, I started training government Job Centre workers in how to run open courses for jobseekers. Finding myself training others in the skills I myself had used a few years previously, it struck me anew how extremely useful these methods were, and how much appreciated they were by those working with disorientated unemployed people. For many coaches and careers advisers, it was exactly the tool they needed in order to deal with people in a respectful way while at the same time effectively supporting them towards resolving their situation.

Most professionals working in this field agree that it is people's attitude that is the determining factor, but there are not many who act according to this basic assumption. The purpose of this book is to encourage more to do so.

I know that those people who have been coached using this method are treated with respect and provided with the conditions in which they can find their own solutions and achieve the kind of life they want, both emotionally and financially. My hope is that this book will be a useful tool for all those who work in a profession which provides support to people.

Karin Tenelius

MY PERSONAL OUTLOOK AND PHILOSOPHY

In order to be able to create the opportunity for jobseekers to change their outlook from a negative one to a productive, positive one, you must be prepared to talk openly and frankly with them. If your coaching style is to be experienced as empowering, and so translated into positive action, it has to be based on the following values:

- People have much greater capacity than they actually make use of. People are capable and competent, and it only takes the right environment for their potential to reveal itself.
- When people regard themselves as accountable for how their lives turn out, they are much better able to create the conditions for getting what they want.
- People have the right to choose how they want to live their lives and what actions they will take, with all the consequences that flow from that.
- People want to feel useful. Nobody wants to be dependent on welfare benefits.
- It is always possible for people to transform their lives.
- The outcomes people get, in all aspects of life, are a direct function of who and how they are.
- A change of attitude leads to a change of outcome.

I am aware that my coaching method is not always obvious compared with current norms of practice. Some people feel that the method I teach is too impersonal, expressing a cold-heartedness and lack of empathy towards my fellow humans. This criticism has never come from the people I coach! It has come from others, often those who work in the care professions.
   It is not possible to coach using my methods without being empathic and treating people with respect, so I am sometimes a bit puzzled by the criticism I receive. Thinking about the reason for it, I have come to the conclusion that it is unusual in our culture to be honest and frank. People associate candid feedback with being unpleasant, believing people cannot handle such directness. Empathy and compassion get confused with

pity and commiseration, which can seem like the right thing to express when someone is going through a rough time. If you do not pity people, but rather if you listen with empathy and do not accept that the person's situation is necessarily hopeless, that is seen by some as wrong, as altogether too unfeeling. My experience is that in our culture we are really bad at recognising the potential and greatness in each other when times are hard.

I hope that my methodology will not be perceived as cold-hearted or lacking in empathy, when in fact it is based on the values and principles set out above.

THE VALUE OF COACHING JOBSEEKERS

In traditional support services, for example within the fields of employment and social work, coaching can lead to more tangible results than more traditional methods, and can have a more sustainable impact on those who seek advice or help. Traditional advisory services within the job market sector are often based on the assumption that it is simply knowledge or skills that are lacking, and so the individual is offered retraining, re-skilling and further education programmes. But because this approach is not based upon whether the person ultimately finds work or not, it is often ineffective and the impact is short-term and unsustainable. Research has also shown that many such programmes fail to produce results and can even be counterproductive.

I believe that it is defining the problem in terms of lack of skill that is wrong. Rather, I would argue that what determines whether someone gets a job, or not, is their attitude to the opportunities on the job market, how they view their own abilities, how they regard potential employers, their overall attitude to work, the extent to which they feel they have something to offer and whether they are counting on finding work through someone else's charity.

A person's attitude to their own barriers also plays a key role. Most people claim that they are either too old or too young for the job market, that they are either over- or under-qualified, their children are too young and so on. According to them, their circumstances are just wrong. Whatever the perceived disadvantage, the individual sees it as an insurmountable obstacle, even though prospective employers do not see it that way. Different people view their life circumstances, experience or age differently. These are barriers that you cannot do much about. The key instead is to change your attitude towards them.

All these attitudes determine one's odds in the job market. So it is about breaking away from, and questioning, your assumptions and preconceptions in order to see new opportunities and embrace new approaches. Coaching in groups or individually helps the participant recognise their resistance, which may be due to lack of self-esteem, fear of contact with customers, an inability to communicate what they have to offer, a tendency to procrastinate and so on. As participants become more conscious of what is standing in their way, they can tackle their resistance and try new approaches and new patterns of behaviour, which in turn will produce different results. What is needed in order to achieve this is that the jobseeker shifts their attitude and approach towards, for example, the possibility of creating their own job opportunity (i.e. moving from the impossible to the possible), or towards focusing on themselves and their own abilities (i.e. moving from expecting someone else to find them a job to concentrating on what they themselves have to offer) and so on. Taken altogether, these changes in a person's thought patterns contribute to a change in that person's behaviour and 'way of being' and, consequently, the chance of success increases immensely.

How does one set about changing a person's attitude? The answer is as simple as it is hard to grasp. Raise awareness! By helping a person to become aware of, and question, their attitudes – while maintaining respect for the individual's choices – whole new perspectives surface. Together with the coach, the person can then examine these new insights and from there can consider new ways of thinking and new starting-points. It can often be painful to abandon established assumptions, because they were in fact serving some purpose. However, when a person sees that there is something to be gained from changing their viewpoint, the choice becomes clearer. The way to achieve this is through a coaching dialogue which has a clear purpose and aim, developed in conjunction with the jobseeker. If the dialogue takes place as part of a government requirement (as is often the case today) as opposed to being purely supportive, the outcome can be counterproductive. For the dialogue to be successful, the jobseeker coach must have adopted a true coaching approach, which I will describe in greater detail in a later section.

Something else that can be gained from coaching the jobseeker is, of course, that if the individual creates their own solution, then the outcome is more sustainable than if the answer had been handed to them on a plate. Moreover, when an individual develops the capacity to drive and carry through their job search for themselves, then these skills, once learned, can be reapplied should they ever find themselves unemployed again. Having once resolved a problem themselves, a person will have more confidence in their ability to do it again.

One further advantage of coaching jobseekers is that it frees up time. The coaching method I describe does not involve an endless succession of follow-up meetings. A skilled coach needs only a few sessions. Once the jobseeker's own potential is released, they can proceed independently to direct their own job search.

AIM OF THE BOOK

This book is primarily intended for people who work in coaching for the job market, for example recruitment agents, project leaders in various job-seeking schemes, social workers, supervisors in government programmes, coaches in rehabilitation and re-employment schemes, as well as freelance coaches whose main interest is the field of employment. I recommend that anyone who is completely new to coaching completes a foundation course first.

The book is intended for use by jobseeker coaches in the following three ways:

- as an introduction aimed at raising interest in the subject
- as background material, training manual and reference for those working towards developing coaching skills
- as in-depth advanced material for existing coaches who want to enhance their proficiency.

The book focuses on practical application rather than discussing theories and theoretical arguments. Coaching is a craft, a skill, a behavioural art – not a theoretical topic. Knowing about the theory of coaching does not make you into a good coach. Just like a windsurfer, you have to be able to stay upright on the board, steer with the sail and be prepared to land in the water many times before you can get the hang of it. Let me make it clear once and for all: to be able to coach someone to achieve, within a short time, the transformation they want is an art. It is about developing the ability to conduct dialogues which bring about change, and this can only be achieved after extensive training.

I find it gratifying that the phenomenon of coaching has become accessible and accepted within the worlds of business and development, because there is great inherent potential in really effective coaching.

But I would also add a word of warning: anyone involved in coaching – whether commissioning, practicing or receiving it – should be aware of the variable quality of services available on the market at present. A problem with coaching is that many think they can do it, without being clear about what real coaching actually entails. In fact, there are very few professional coaches who have training in how to lead a discussion at a level which addresses a person's *attitudes*. Teaching oneself to be a coach through reading a book is about as effective as learning to windsurf by reading a book – it isn't! Despite this, I decided to set down in a book the sum of my knowledge and skill in coaching jobseekers, in order to structure and consolidate those experiences that I have found so useful.

What I want to provide through the book are the practical skills I teach coaches in the training I deliver. If you want to use the book to its best advantage and achieve concrete results, you will have to start working hard at putting the methods described into practice, quite simply adopting them as your own. I have often heard the participants on my courses grumbling about how incredibly difficult it is to become a good coach, because the more you learn the more you find there is to learn. But if you have the talent for, and interest in, coaching and you are prepared to put in the effort and above all be open to frank feedback, it is one of the most enjoyable and amazing careers. Your reward is to be able to help people take full responsibility for themselves and their lives in the realisation of their dreams, which in the long run – believe it or not! – will contribute to making the world a better place.

CONTENTS

The book contains 10 sections. It is intended as a text book, beginning with the basic concepts of coaching and gradually becoming more advanced. It can also be used as a reference manual for anyone confronted with a dilemma in a coaching situation.

In the first section, I explore the distinction between coaching as a way of 'doing' and as a way of 'being'. I also explain the significance of the five attitudes which together make up a true coaching approach. In the second section, I discuss the basic skills which one must develop in order to be able to conduct a coaching dialogue, to coach at the so-called 'issue level'. The third section deals amongst other things with the basic requirements that have to be fulfilled in order to be able to start coaching, and how these can be acquired. The fourth section is possibly the most important in the whole book, dealing as it does with attitude-based coaching. Not until you have mastered this will your coaching be truly effective. Section five summarises some common challenges when you are acting in the capacity of both government official and coach, and discusses how to deal with the negative attitudes that those who are unemployed typically tend to have. In the sixth section, I describe some effective tools and in the seventh I give examples of what good coaching can achieve. How to coach groups is covered in section eight, and section nine offers a collection of hints and tips to develop one's training. The book concludes with section ten, in which I answer some common questions as well as demonstrating how to deal with the challenges that I will set out shortly.

Translator's note

In the English text, the word 'attitude' is used to encompass also the sense of 'mindset', 'frame of mind', 'personal approach', 'outlook' etc.

The word 'productive' in the context of 'productive attitude' is used to capture a sense of 'fruitful', 'constructive', 'favourable' and 'advantageous'. Similarly, 'unproductive' denotes 'unfruitful', 'unconstructive', 'unfavourable' and 'disadvantageous'.

For simplicity, in the English text, the informal 'they', 'their' etc. is used to denote 'he or she', 'his or her' etc.

SOME COMMON CHALLENGES WHEN COACHING JOBSEEKERS

Supporting people who are unemployed, and who in many cases have not even sought help, is a challenging task. Below are some examples of common questions I am confronted with when training coaches. Keep these questions in mind as you read the book, as I will revisit them at the end.

- How can I motivate someone who has simply given up?
- How do I coach spoilt young people who do not want to do anything at all?
- What can I do about someone who hides behind health problems, even though they are not officially registered as sick?
- How do I get a person over 55 to want to get a job?
- What do I do about someone who does not accept that they are just too choosy?
- How do I get someone to relocate to find work?
- What do I do when even I think someone is a hopeless case?

SECTION 1

COACHING AS A WAY OF 'BEING' RATHER THAN 'DOING'

WHAT EXACTLY IS COACHING ALL ABOUT?

There are many descriptions and definitions of coaching. For me, coaching is about empowering a person to achieve their desired aim. It is a 'way of being', which helps another person draw on their potential. This may seem like rather an abstract definition until you have practiced as a coach yourself and discovered what coaching is, and is not, about. To return to the analogy of windsurfing, you cannot understand the skill involved until you suddenly grasp how to get your balance and let the wind take the sail.

First of all, every coaching experience is totally unique and if you are not a trained coach, or have not received effective coaching, then you have never truly experienced it. It means you have nothing to compare it with, no frame of reference. You may think you understand, but you don't really. Just think about all those managers who think they are great coaches while their colleagues beg to differ!

Secondly, coaching is more an approach than simply a method. It is more about *who you are* than what you do and say. You might say all the right things and still be unsuccessful, and vice versa.

In a way, it is easier to describe what coaching is *not*. Coaching is not a pep talk. It is not about cheering someone up or encouraging them, as some may think. Of course it is desirable that people feel encouraged, but merely encouraging them seldom brings about a sustainable outcome. It starts from the assumption that the coach's energy, inspiration and motivation will rub off on the person being coached, when in fact such inspiration is short-lived and is insufficient to deal with the issue that needs to be tackled.

> The purpose of coaching is to empower another person to achieve their desired aim. Coaching is a 'way of being' which enables another person to choose to draw on their own potential.

Neither is coaching about being served up with ready-made solutions, sterling advice or handy tips by someone more experienced. In other words, it is not about transferring your knowledge to another. It is not mentorship, in the sense of a more experienced and knowledgeable person sharing their advice and expertise.

Coaching involves a trained coach actively listening to a person in a way that enables that person to find their own answers and solutions. The coach conducts a dialogue which enables the jobseeker to access and draw on their own resources and start acting in a different way. The coach becomes a catalyst, not merely adding their own input but acting as a tool to create a dialogue which releases the potential inherent in the other person. Coaching also involves reflecting back to the jobseeker, asking penetrating questions and giving feedback which can lead to whole new insights into problems and challenges and provide a new starting-point from which to base one's actions.

In the following sections I will define the coaching 'way of being' and describe the approaches you need to take in order to achieve it.

GOOD COACHING IS A PRODUCT OF WHO YOU ARE

As I said above, good coaching is not so much a product of what you *do* – the questions you ask and topics you raise – as in who you *are* when you coach, how you behave in your role. Active listening, which is central to coaching, is not something you do, but a frame of mind, a way of being.

Coaches who have mastered this approach automatically empower others around them, making them quickly feel that they have the coach's full attention and interest. That is why when I train coaches I do not teach them a methodology. I do not focus so much on, for example, the structure of their conversations as I do on who they are when they coach. And who they are when coaching is determined by their approach.

When I first started training coaches, I identified five attitudes or mindsets which together make up a coaching approach. Training as a coach involves developing these five attitudes. To have a coaching approach, you need to integrate them into your way of being. Of course this should not be at the cost of your own basic personality. Our attitudes essentially reflect our values and have nothing to do with our personality type. You are who you are, but you have to be prepared to work on those attitudes of yours that may be holding you back from adopting a true coaching approach. The process is mainly about identifying your weaknesses, in other words which of the five attitudes you find it most difficult to assimilate when engaging in the coaching dialogue. Most of my trainee coaches can quickly identify one or two that are the key stumbling blocks for them. The training to a large extent therefore involves becoming increasingly conscious of these 'traps' so as to avoid falling into them.

FIVE ATTITUDES OF A GOOD COACH

The five attitudes which together make up a coaching approach are:
- Relating to people's potential
- Understanding the limits of your responsibility
- Clarifying and summarising
- Accepting the situation as it is
- Not having your own agenda.

You may think that these five points seem simple and obvious, or perhaps they say nothing to you at all. Whichever it is, I would argue that when a coach integrates these five attitudes into their practice, it will result in people being able to achieve real change.

The task for you as a trainee coach is to embrace these attitudes, understanding their characteristics and starting to determine which you have already integrated and which still remain a challenge for you.

RELATING TO PEOPLE'S POTENTIAL

I am certain that anyone working with people will agree that it is crucial to be able to recognise and relate to the inherent potential and capacity in others. This is the basis of our work. However, my experience is that while it sounds good in theory, it is harder to put into practice. It is not easy to continue seeing someone as capable and competent when they are for the moment not tapping into their potential. In such cases, it is easier to give up and, more or less subconsciously, regard the person as a helpless. Then we try to help, to compensate for their helplessness by using our own strength on their behalf.

So the question is: how to relate to the jobseeker. Consider the following two statements:

1) It is easy to relate to people as capable beings if we ourselves believe them capable.

2) It is hard to relate to people as capable beings if we do not believe them to be capable.

When people find themselves unemployed, their potential is not always visible. There may be many reasons for this, for example that they have turned the setbacks into a given fact that they will never succeed, that they are not good enough. A person's attitude can affect their inner potential, but cannot make it disappear! It remains a hidden resource which can at any time be activated once the person feels sufficiently motivated. Tapping into our inherent capacity may involve taking risks, something we are not always prepared to do. Whether we choose to make use of our potential often depends on whether we think there is sufficient value in the possible outcome and that it is therefore worth investing in the unavoidable risk-taking. This is usually an unconscious thought process for most people. As a coach, it is your job to clarify such thought processes and provide the opportunity for the jobseeker to access their inner resources. So this also involves clarifying what investment they will have to make in the process and enabling them to calculate the risks involved, so that they can make a decision and choose their approach.

Crucial to your success as a coach is that you at all times relate to the jobseeker as a capable individual. A possible trap for you is that you more or less unconsciously slip into a mode where you see the jobseeker as needing help, ideas, advice, a mother, a police officer, a carer or a project leader. You know best which of these roles most applies to you. Without realising what you are doing, you may subconsciously think: "this isn't going to work", "he's a hopeless case", "…a victim of circumstance", "…all talk and no action", "…a useless waster", or something along these lines.

Of course, your perception of the person in front of you is valid. But the problem is that your inner dialogue and thoughts affect you in a way that is adverse to a coaching way of being. It may only last a few seconds or it may creep more and more into each meeting you have with the person.

To illustrate what I believe, I will tell you what a friend of mine used to say:

> "When I'm with some people I become smart, I have insight and can come up with the most brilliant ideas: but with other people I just become muddled and confused, always putting my foot in it. When I meet certain people, I feel witty. People laugh and I develop a sort of comic timing. And when I meet others, I just become stupid, trying to be funny but just coming over as pathetic. In short, when I meet some people I can access my inner strength, when I'm with others I'm about as far from being able to do that as you can get. Who I become is a function of how others see me, how they relate to me, and whether they recognise my potential or not."

To recognise and relate to someone's potential does not mean you have to believe in their pipedreams, or sit and listen to them going over and over why everything is impossible, or wait for a miracle to happen to that unmotivated 23-year-old sitting before you. To relate to someone's potential is to truly believe that the 'sack of hay' sitting before you already has the capacity needed to achieve the seemingly impossible – in other words, to find a job.

Training as a coach helps develop in you the ability to address yourself consistently to a person's maximum potential, not their shortcomings. It involves talking adult to adult, not like a parent, a person in authority or a do-gooder. When you really and truly believe in the person you are working with, you open the door to all kinds of possibilities. Competent or incompetent? – try it yourself! How you relate to the person in front of you will determine the outcome.

Another aspect of trusting in the jobseeker's own inner resources is that you are able to accept that they can tolerate you being frank with them. If you are coaching someone with unrealistic dreams, such as a 47 year old who wants to be a fighter pilot, you need to start talking straight to them about their tendency to fantasise, rather than get into an argument about whether or not it is possible to become a fighter pilot at the age of 47.

Here is another example. Perhaps deep down you know that one of your jobseekers is not going to get a job because no employer is going to tolerate that 'know-it-all' attitude of theirs, which you yourself have had to endure in meetings and group sessions. In this case you have to politely but firmly, and with all seriousness, feed back to them how their attitude is holding them back.

People can handle straight talking. Receiving frank feedback gives people the means to make a positive change. In order to develop, people need to acknowledge the different sides of their character. That does not mean there is something inherently wrong with the individual, only that the jobseeker – just like you and I – has their more and less positive sides. In fact, I would contend that to talk straight is to show respect, and everyone who accepts straight talking feels respected.

You probably agree with the above statement. But do you dare examine yourself for a moment and consider the following question: have there never been occasions when you have thought, "Oh no! Not her again!" or "Not another meeting with him!" It is not wrong or inappropriate to have such thoughts, but the important thing is to be aware that you are thinking like that and that it could negate your ability to coach. The solution is not to force yourself to think positively about the person but to use your perceptions as a tool in your coaching. For example, you might say, "You know what? I just realised that I've given up on you. I'm telling you this straight, because if you're going to succeed, we need to talk about what is *really* holding you back. And what is holding you back is that you're full of talk but there's no action."

> **People can handle straight talking. Being given frank feedback is a means to positive development.**

If you are going to continue coaching this person, then you have to be prepared to examine your own perspectives and consider the possibility that the person you have before you has potential. It is just that it is not obvious at the moment. If you cannot do this, then discontinue the coaching, because now it is your view of the jobseeker that is the greatest obstacle to their progress!

UNDERSTANDING THE LIMITS OF YOUR RESPONSIBILITY

You have one single area of responsibility as a coach, and that is to ensure that the dialogue is productive, that it progresses in such a way that the person you are coaching is given the opportunity to create the outcome they want. The jobseeker is responsible for everything else – their job search, their life, their family, their personal finances and their dog. When coaching jobseekers, there is a tendency for the person to transfer their responsibilities onto the coach. It can sound like this:

"Have you arranged any work practice for me yet?"

"What do you think I should do, then?"

"Why should I come here if you can't offer me a job?"

Often the transfer of responsibility comes as early as 30 seconds into the conversation. The trap lies in you failing to point out that the jobseeker has just tried to push the responsibility onto you. The coach who has already fallen into the trap continues to discuss the job search as if nothing has happened – with the difference that the responsibility is now laying in the coach's lap.

Another sign that you have assumed too much responsibility is when you start to steer the conversation. You behave as if you are driving the process and the jobseeker is merely a passenger who 'goes along for the ride'. You present an overview of the jobseeker's task, even though that is for them to do, and you jump in with suggestions for action. Any silences in the conversation are broken by you. In short, you are doing too much and taking the wrong approach. One reason for this is that you believe you should deliver something or achieve a result. You won't! It is the person you are coaching who will find a job. It is their responsibility. The fact is that if you take over control from the person (which may not even be what they want) then you are robbing them of every chance of getting a job. When you assume responsibility, the jobseeker tends to become 'small' and passive, while you want to take responsibility and show how 'big' you are. Your job is to hand back all the responsibility that is not yours, stepping back from your assumed role as leader of the job search.

It is the jobseeker's own task to reach their goal, regardless of the circumstances. The worse the job market situation, the more responsibility the jobseeker has to take. To sit back and hope that the economic situation will improve is to be a victim of circumstance.

> **Step down from your role as project leader!**

Silences during the conversation can be particularly difficult to deal with. Yet these have an important function, for when you are silent you allow the other person to take control. Do not fill silences with activity, when there is no activity in the conversation. If you find it difficult to remain silent, it is a sign that you are taking too much responsibility. Your coaching style needs to change to become more 'cool' and laid back, while of course at the same time remaining engaged.

If, as coach, you try to use the force of your will to get an individual onto the 'right track', or offer solutions, then you will create resistance in the jobseeker. The desire to find

> **Learning to feel comfortable with silence is a prerequisite for good coaching.**

solutions has to come from the jobseeker, without your unasked-for advice.

If you recognise this as being a major stumbling-block for you, you are probably an energising, inspiring coach, full of ideas and inspiration. You just have a tendency to take over when you coach. What is driving you to do that? Is it perhaps the kind of thoughts illustrated on next page? If that is so, it might be worth examining them more closely.

As I mentioned earlier, it is not you, the coach, that is expected to come up with answers, and this explains why it is so difficult to resist taking on responsibility. What drives us to inappropriately assume responsibility is often a fear of not performing, of wanting to be efficient and look good. To avoid looking unsuccessful, we take responsibility, ensure we have control and try to make sure we do not fail.

> **Stop being a total achiever!**

If you experience a jobseeker as lacking in energy and drive, it is also easy to start compensating by showing drive and energy yourself. But for the person you are coaching to be successful, you have to relinquish control, avoid taking responsibility and quite simply have confidence that things will work out.

Here are some examples of the questions that can help you stop taking responsibility:

"How do you want to use our time together today?"

"What do you want the outcome of our meeting today to be?"

"What is the next step in your job search?"

"You say you don't know. If you don't know, who do you think might have the answer?"

"I hear you say that you can't do it, but if you could ...?"

"There aren't many jobs of that kind on the market, so how are you going to deal with that?"

"How do you think you can make progress in the world as it is, when there are no jobs of that kind available?"

When I first start talking to trainee coaches about the issue of responsibility, and the need to train jobseekers from the outset to come to the session ready to make use of the coach rather than just coming along to 'be coached', they usually smile and ask: "Have you ever actually met someone who has been made redundant, Karin? That approach doesn't work with the kinds of people we coach."

I usually challenge them to try it out, and after a couple of weeks they all realise that it is their own tendency to take responsibility that determines how the conversation develops. All coaching dialogues

> **Taking over responsibility for someone else's job search means you disqualify the person from being project leader in their own project.**

COACHING JOBSEEKERS 31

should begin with "How do you want to make use of me today?", and this should feel perfectly natural for both the coach and the jobseeker. If you have the inclination to take on too much responsibility, you need to let go of your urge to offer solutions and to take over the job search.

CLARIFYING AND SUMMARISING

Your task as a coach is, together with the jobseeker, to clarify and elucidate – without giving advice, tips or solutions – that which stands in the way or are the thing that is lacking in order for the jobseeker to achieve what they want to achieve.

The basic position here is not to add you own input into the process but merely to bring issues to the surface and raise awareness. You act as a catalyst and empower the jobseeker by clarifying, for example, their current situation, the choices before them and any unproductive attitudes they may have. You do not need any specialist skills other than the ability to coach. It is *not* your job to impart new knowledge or skills to your jobseeker. To do that is to prevent good coaching. One exception may be when the jobseeker is begging you for advice – only then may you give it. Otherwise giving advice, tips and solutions is generally counterproductive, and a trap that is very easy to fall into.

We are overconfident that the other person will take up our suggestions and ideas, as if that is all that is missing. But if you start to take note of how many of your hints and tips are taken on board and result in a positive outcome, you would be shocked at how few actually are. I know that this is hard to accept for many working in the fields of counselling and support services, but I would ask you to consider this: giving advice stands in the way of effective coaching.

> Giving advice stands in the way of effective coaching.

Above all, you should never try to transfer your own competences, your own energy and strength to the person you are coaching. It is your job to release theirs. In practice it may feel like your verbal input is a bit curtailed, as if you are only making observations on the situation. For example, you may say, "I notice that every time you come here you have changed track", rather than make a non-coaching comment such as: "You have to make up your mind. I recommend the first alternative." Or you may say: "I hear that you plan to establish one new contact next week. To me that doesn't sound like enough. What do you think?" instead of the more directive: "You have to make at least four new contacts next week."

If you spot yourself in this trap, it probably means that your coaching technique is over-reliant on you in offering advice, tips and solutions. To put it bluntly, you love giving advice. The painful truth is that, in order to improve your coaching skills, you need to put aside all your hot tips and bright ideas and simply trust that change will happen without them. Eliminate advice and tips from your vocabulary. Cut back on your opinions and just make observations and statements. That is the only way to transfer the responsibility to the person who actually has to find the job. Clarifying, for example, the facts of the situation or the barriers in the way of progress makes the jobseeker aware of things that were not previously apparent to them. This empowers them. Here is an example:

Coach: It sounds to me like you've let the circumstances determine your actions so far.

Jobseeker: Yes, maybe I have. I didn't see it like that before but you're probably right. So it's not really surprising that I haven't been able to make things work out, is that what you mean?

When you learn to summarise and clarify rather than jump in with your own solutions, you release a huge amount of creativity and acceptance of responsibility in your jobseeker. You do not have to do the work yourself – and that is the point! Relax and concentrate on having a dialogue which is productive and brings about change, rather than trying to solve other people's problems.

ACCEPTING THE SITUATION AS IT IS

This attitude is about freeing yourself up from thinking in terms of 'right' and 'wrong' and keeping your own views and values in check in order to coach well. It is a matter of meeting people on their own ground, accepting their attitude and behaviour without reacting to it. By taking this approach you will contribute towards achieving change. You will never be able to get someone from A to B if you cannot take them along with you. Every individual is where they are. As a coach you have to give up trying to create a shift in the jobseeker – they have to use their own power to create a shift, and that can only happen if you accept things as they are. If a person is allowed to be where they are and who they are, they will feel accepted and respected and will thereby be able to start working on finding their own way forward without you pulling them in a particular direction.

The pitfall in relation to this approach can manifest itself in your trying to cheer the jobseeker up, give them a pep talk, to compensate for their lack of initiative. Perhaps you will become the driver and take control yourself. If you are in an official government role, it is easy to hide behind 'rules and regulations': "you *have to* be actively seeking work to qualify for benefits" or "a jobseeker shouldn't behave like that". This is not a true coaching approach and is consequently counterproductive. If you adopt this approach, there is a great risk that the jobseeker will start to work against you rather than with you. Notice that here I am talking about how you *are* as a coach, not what you *say*. It is not so much about your comments as your outlook, your attitude. In the above example, you would seem to be suggesting that the jobseeker should pull themselves together and make an effort. (The section on *Mixed roles – coach and government employee* on page 92 goes into more detail on how to deal with mixed roles.)

There is also an illusion that if the coach accepts the jobseeker's feelings of resignation, then the resigned state will become permanent. But this is not so. If you can accept feelings of resignation, then the person themselves can start to work towards a different, more constructive state of mind, without the need for you to 'cheer them up'. Believe it or not, the paradoxical truth is that accepting that someone has given up, for example, is the most productive thing you can do. It frees up all the potential within the person themselves to create the desired outcome.

> **As a coach, accepting the jobseeker's feelings of resignation is the most productive thing you can do.**

Look instead at yourself. You have to be able to be in the presence of someone who is feeling hopeless without intervening. When you are there for them in their present frame of mind, without expecting a result, then results are achieved. So what can you do instead? You can simply be there and reflect back the state of mind in which they find themselves. It may sound like this:

> "You think things are looking bleak for you."
>
> "You're feeling as if you've given up."
>
> "It sounds as if you can't see any ways out."

Just to be there, acknowledge the other person and reflect back to them their thoughts, feelings and frame of mind is actually all that is needed. You will be astonished how much positive energy this approach can generate.

NOT HAVING YOUR OWN AGENDA

When you are coaching, it is not your agenda that should steer the process. You may have plans and good ideas for the person you are coaching, but it is only their ambitions and aims that should steer the coaching situation. You act as a catalyst so that they can realise their own goals for themselves. To act in that way, you need to keep your own plans and ideas to yourself. As a coach it is not your job to put these forward – that is not good coaching. This can be really challenging for those of you who have to meet a demand for results from superiors. The trick is to trust that the jobseeker has an aim and agenda that match yours. If this is not the case, then coaching someone in a job search is not relevant, and the sessions should be discontinued. Remember – coaching can only be successful if you are able to align yourself with the jobseeker's own goals. In other words, coaching can never be successful when it is based on someone else's agenda.

But what if the jobseeker's goal is not to find a job? Well, if the person in question really doesn't want to get a job, then it is pointless to continue working as a jobseeker coach, no matter whether you work as an employment consultant, a government Job Centre official or a supervisor in a retraining scheme. What you can do in these circumstance is to take up the dilemma with your jobseeker in a calm, friendly and matter of fact way, without becoming indignant or interrogating them. For example, you might say:

"You don't seem to be focused on looking for a job."

"You don't seem to be doing anything about finding a job."

"Describe to me what your real aim is."

"What exactly do you want to be coached in?"

"How do you want to make use of this coaching session?"

"What is it you want to achieve?"

"What was it you were imagining?"

My experience, however, is that for the vast majority of people who are out of work, finding a job is their real goal. There are many possible reasons why there are an increasing number who do not seem to want to work, and this will be dealt with in a later section, *The Basic Preconditions for Coaching.* (see page 59).

A common trap when coaching is that you have a more or less unconscious plan for the jobseeker, which makes your discussions like a designated path down which you try to lead them. Recognise the temptation to do this and let go of your own agenda!

> **Coaching a jobseeker will never be successful if it is based on an agenda other than the jobseeker's.**

DEVELOPING A COACHING APPROACH – INTEGRATING THE FIVE ATTITUDES

To start training yourself to achieve a coaching approach, you need to thoroughly explore the 5 attitudes set out above. Tackle the ones you feel cause you most difficulty. Discuss them with someone else who is interested in coaching, so that you get someone else's view on the traps you need to look out for.

If your weakness is that you can't relate to the potential in others, condition yourself to delegate more often than you would usually do. Pay attention to how you regard the people around you and how you assess their abilities. For example, practice with your children. Would they be able to do more for themselves if you weren't holding their hand all the time? How do you really judge other people's competence? Who, according to you, is capable? Who isn't? When did you assume the right to judge other people's abilities?

If your weakness is that you take too much responsibility, make a list of all the things you see as your responsibility which aren't really. Then for the next week relinquish responsibility for half of them and see what happens – try to observe whether people around you regard you as irresponsible. Relax and don't be afraid. In your coaching try to notice which of the people you coach you feel most responsible for. Put the ball back in their court: hand back the responsibility in your next meeting.

If your weakness is that you tend to give advice, tips and solutions instead of clarifying and summarising, then note how many hints and tips you spout in a week. If you want to keep a tally, give yourself one penalty point for each piece of advice you give. Notice also what the outcome is when you give advice. Try instead to be silent and listen. Ask a friend or colleague to coach you in a role-play where you discuss a pressing dilemma or problem. Ask your friend to dish out lots of advice and reflect on how it felt to you.

If your weakness is that you find it difficult to accept things as they are, train yourself to become more open to alternatives. Observe what sort of person you become when you begin to feel that you can't accept a situation, or when you feel that the jobseeker 'should' behave differently, should be more effective or improve in some way. Seek situations which you normally tend to avoid, and observe your own reactions and actions.

If your weakness is that you find it difficult to let go of your own agenda, train yourself to *ask more questions*, such as: "What is it you want?"; "How do you want to proceed/do this?"; "What do you suggest?" Ask your children, your partner, people you meet during your working day etc. If you are chairing meetings, ask the other participants: "What do you think are the most important issues we need to discuss today?"

A sign that you may have fallen into a trap can be an almost physical reaction. You may feel physical symptoms, such as a dry throat, exaggerated gestures, a tendency to lean forward towards those you are speaking to etc. Learn to recognise these physical signals when you fall into a trap during a conversation. Being aware of them means you can choose to get out of the trap. If your weakness is that you tend to take too much responsibility, or dominate the conversation by leading or directing, you usually lean forward while talking to your jobseeker. If you usually compensate by offering too much advice, you may find that your mouth becomes dry from talking so much. If your weakness is that you find it difficult to accept the situation as it is, it is quite possible that the effort you are making will make you feel warm and perspire.

SECTION 2
TRADITIONAL ISSUE-BASED COACHING

COACHING THAT DEALS WITH ISSUES COMPARED WITH ATTITUDE

This section deals primarily with two basic and essential abilities during the coaching dialogue: to listen and to ask questions. They belong in that order because the absolutely most important coaching skill of all is the ability to listen. Once you have mastered these two skills, you can base your coaching conversations on issues. That is to say, you will be able to actively offer support to your jobseeker so that they will be in a position to analyse and understand their present dilemma, and so be able to go forward.

Since many jobseekers feel 'stuck' and unable to break out of the unproductive frame of mind that is preventing them from reaching their goal, then so-called issue-based coaching is not going to be sufficient in order to achieve results. But to listen and ask questions are not just important foundations for the coaching conversation. To be able to listen enables you to take up subjects that are not being openly stated and to identify any unproductive attitudes and behaviours. This is what I call attitude-based coaching and I will return to it in Section 4.

BASIC COACHING SKILLS

LISTENING

Let us start with the basics of being a good listener. A necessary starting-point is to assume that you are not at the moment using your listening ability to the extent that you could. Most of us believe we are good at listening, but we do not come near to what is possible. Since training yourself to listen is not as practical an exercise as, for example, learning how to play the piano, you have to be personally motivated to want to learn to be better at listening, otherwise it is not easy to get started.

> **Be aware that you're not really listening!**

One way of increasing your motivation is to get an idea of how the people around you judge your listening skills – their feedback may contain some very unpleasant truths. When I started my own training many years ago, I wasn't very happy to be told that I had a habit of completing other people's sentences for them, and it meant I missed a lot of what they were saying. I realised that I actually wasn't listening to them at all! It was hard to acknowledge, but very good at motivating me to quickly change my behaviour. Today I hear myself when I fall into my old habits and can change my behaviour so that I can keep listening.

If you have children, they are a great ready source of information. Ask them how you act when you are not listening to them. You will probably be given a crystal clear description that will make you blush and which reveals all the traps you have to start tackling. If you don't have children, just ask your partner. If you don't have a partner, ask your closest friends. As a complement to this exercise, you can reflect on the statements on the following page, but make sure to use them as supplemental to, not instead of, the feedback from others.

Exercise 1

Read the statements below and notice which ones most strike you. They give important clues as to where the key traps for you lie when it comes to listening. If after reading them you say, "These are all pitfalls for me", then that is a pitfall in itself. The value for you comes in being specific and really being concrete about one or two from the list.

- I don't listen to the end. I jump in and fill in what I think the other person is going to say.
- While I'm listening, I'm also wondering what the other person thinks of me. (I feel like I have to perform.)
- My thoughts often drift to what I see as the most relevant bit of the conversation or the part I associate with most.
- I listen more in order to be able to provide an answer, rather than to understand.
- When the topic of conversation interests me, I wait for the other person to stop talking so that I can say my bit.
- I think in advance about what I want to say next.
- I concentrate so much on appearing interested that I hardly hear a word.
- I lose concentration if the other person talks for too long, or if I'm not interested in the subject.
- I try to listen even when I don't actually have the time.
- I keep thinking about whether what the person is saying seems logical or illogical, right or wrong, true or false.
- I listen most to the spoken words and don't take in the tone of voice, the body language or facial expressions.
- If I get impatient, I interrupt.
- I am easily distracted by things around me.

Once you have picked out your key stumbling-blocks when you are listening, think about which situations usually make you fall into these patterns of not listening. What sorts of people do you tend to listen to least? How do you usually behave in these situations?

Now the work starts to observe on a daily basis when you have ended up in a trap. In other words, be conscious of it and then choose a different way of behaving to your usual one. The more you dare to acknowledge the traps – in other words, the more feedback you accept and the clearer your patterns of behaviour become – the easier it will be for you to be aware of them and change them.

In order to remember to keep being attentive to your way of listening, you could put up reminders to support yourself, for example a note saying "How am I listening?" on the door of your fridge or on your screen saver. If there are others in your workplace who are coaches, ask them continually for feedback. Ask them to tell you when you fall into a trap if you happen to do so at coffee break. Anyone who has previously given you feedback can keep giving you reminders. If you are supporting someone in a coaching conversation, reflect extra carefully upon your listening skills during the session.

Exercise 2

A useful tool is the 'parroting' technique, which involves you repeating back what the other person says, using their own words. Again, if you have children, try this on them – they'll love it!

Example:

Child: I made three paper kites at school today, Dad!

Dad: Oh, so you made three paper kites at school today!

Child: Yes, a blue one, a green one and a pink one. The pink one was the best!

Dad: I see. One blue kite, one green kite, and the best one – the pink one.

Child: Yes, and it was really difficult to cut them out. Anna helped to get the tails right.

Dad: I see. They were difficult to cut out, especially the tails, so Anna helped you.

As a parent you are normally bored to death after the first statement and parroting is a real pain. But believe me, this exercise can have magic results in several ways. Partly you come to discover how unused you are to not putting your own contribution into a conversation, and partly you find that the conversation will develop much more than if you block it with your comments. Try it!

Exercise 3

The following is a variation on the previous exercise. Have a conversation with someone where you only summarise what the other person says, after each time they have spoken. Notice how long it takes the other person to move towards their own solution merely by parroting them. Give this technique a try, and try to disregard how silly or pointless it feels just to repeat what someone else has said. You have to be able to overcome this feeling until it feels quite natural to 'just' repeat.

This is a skill that you will be using often during your coaching – not adding your own input, just bringing something to the surface by repeating it. The important thing is that your contributions are totally neutral and free from your own additions, interpretations and conclusions. In order to achieve this, you need to learn to live with being reduced to the role of a 'parrot'.

The result you can expect when you train in this technique is that you hear some unexpected things. People will relate to you in a new way the more you listen, they confide in you more, because a good listener automatically instils trust.

Being 'present' in the situation is at the core of good listening skills. Being 'present' is about consciously rooting yourself in the 'here and now', nowhere else. It is your job to be in the here and now, and disengage yourself from anything else but the person sitting in front of you. Try to disengage your attention from what you should say, in other words from thinking that the thing you want to input is more important than what the jobseeker is saying.

> Being 'present' is at the core of good listening skills.

Being more 'present' starts with you recognising how you are when you are 'present' and when you are 'not present'. Then you will be more aware of your level of presence. From that knowledge you can choose a higher level of engagement.

Listening is a professional skill which you may choose to apply or not, depending on the circumstances, in the same way as any other skill. When we talk about 'listening' in the coaching context, we do not use it in its usual meaning of hearing what another person is saying. It is about listening to what is not said, paying attention to who the other person really is, looking for what is missing, or what it is they are really trying to communicate or achieve – in other words, to listen more for abstract things rather than just spoken words. Without being able to really listen, you can neither formulate useful questions nor give relevant feedback, and the clues to how to do both these lie in what you hear – they're not inside your own head.

ASKING QUESTIONS

When it comes to the ability to ask productive questions, stage one is above all to ask questions, which many people find impossible. Stage two concerns asking those questions which contribute to the progress of the conversation. Training and practising is the only way to master these skills, to find out which questions produce which answers, based on the principle that one gets the answer one deserves. A good coach is able to narrow down any core problem using five or six questions, and then go on working from there. A solution to a complex problem can be found in around 20 to 30 minutes, irrespective of the nature of the problem. This process involves being able to strip away the non-essentials, only listening for the significant information and making it explicit.

The technique is to ask questions, listen to the answers, and then ask new questions based on the responses given, with the overall purpose of clarifying the relevant factors in relation to the desired outcome.

The next question to ask is not already in your head: it is embedded in the answer you have just heard. This can be frustrating at first. You need to learn not to plan your questions in advance. To do this you must develop your listening skills and your ability to accept the situation as it is. The better you become at listening, the easier it will be to identify the obvious question that will lead to positive progress. However, you should really start by experimenting, using a variety of different questions upon which you can reflect and learn. So which questions work, and which do not?

Stop thinking!

When you first start coaching there is a lot of *trial and error* when it comes to asking questions, and that is how it has to be. However, it is important, while you are experimenting, to reflect upon which questions will take things forward and which will not. Trainee coaches are often surprised that their supposedly brilliant questions were not actually so productive. The more you reflect upon your own questions, and the more feedback you ask for, the more skilful you will become. You always need to be open to wanting to be better, even if you are already good.

There are many different types of questions, some of which are productive and positive for coaching, and others which are unproductive and unhelpful in moving the process forward. As with all other areas of coaching training, you must be able to identify your personal traps in order to improve. Here are some examples of unproductive questions:

UNPRODUCTIVE QUESTIONS

Closed questions **often only result in a 'yes' or a 'no' response**
Example: "Did you enjoy the tasks involved in your work?"
The effect of this is that your jobseeker does not have to do any of the work themselves. Practise how to distinguish between open and closed questions. Try asking one open and one closed question at the same stage

of the coaching process and compare the response.
Reflect! What it is you want to achieve by asking that question? What use will you make of the answer?

Leading questions **steer the conversation**
Example: "Have you thought about starting your own business?"
The effect will be that the coach has a possible solution in mind, that the coach will do all the work for the person, when they should actually be doing this themselves. The jobseeker becomes a consumer of advice and tips. Train yourself to stop listening to the ideas and solutions which pop up in your own mind, and focus on listening to the other person.
Reflect! How do you regard the jobseeker and their ability? Do you find it difficult to trust that they are creative and competent?

"Why" questions **are open invitations to historical explanations**
Example: "Why don't you enjoy doing this task?"
The effect of this question is that the coach, in the worst case scenario, will have to listen to the person's entire life story, and this information is irrelevant and useless in relation to the purpose of the coaching task. As a coach, you should never ask "why?". Learn to notice when you ask questions relating to a person's past, and teach yourself to reframe these at the same part of the dialogue.
Reflect! Do you need the whole background story to be able to coach? Consider the notion that you will become a better coach by only working with the present and the future.

Asking for facts **produces unnecessarily detailed answers**
Example: "How long did you work there?"
The outcome of this question is that you will be given a whole lot of information that you do not need, because you are not the one who has to solve the problem. Besides, your question implies that you need this information to be able to draw some clever conclusions, again suggesting that it is you who has to do the work rather than the jobseeker. The questions should be aimed at supporting the jobseeker in their own development, not for gathering background information. As a coach, you need to learn to disregard your apparent need for unnecessary background information. Stop documenting what the other person is saying, and instead start trusting more that the quality of your dialogue will empower the jobseeker.
Reflect! What do you need the information for?

Questions asked purely from your own curiosity **are irrelevant**
Example: "So, you were a researcher. What was it like? What field did you work in? What were your findings?"
The effect of such questions is that they do not contribute to the main purpose of the conversation, and so are pointless. You have become so fascinated by what the jobseeker is telling you that you get sidetracked into something that interests you, instead of making progress. Learn to make the purpose of the conversation explicit, and discipline yourself to stay on track. Ask yourself: "Did any of these questions contribute to moving things forward?"
Reflect! You are probably easily fascinated by other people's stories. How could you satisfy this need in some other way rather than in your coaching sessions?

Too many questions **make engagement impossible**
Here, the coach is so focused on achieving results that the questions are fired out one after the other and do not allow the jobseeker any real chance to answer them.
The effect is that the jobseeker never gets to engage with any one question in any depth. You take over the responsibility from them, when they should be doing the work themselves. Learn to feel comfortable with silence. Ask a question then stay silent for several minutes. Or, if you have to stand up and address a group, start by being silent for 30 seconds.
Reflect! You are driven by the need to achieve, but why? You are not supposed to add *your own input* into the coaching. Consider the idea that your coaching is valuable without you adding anything.

PRODUCTIVE QUESTIONS

Productive questions are those that will contribute to progress and enable things to *move forward*. The following are some examples of these:

Open questions **will produce full answers**
Example: "What do you think about your present situation?"
Open questions are those that cannot be answered simply with "yes" or "no". They are questions which begin with What, Who, How, When, Which.

Follow-up questions **are aimed at developing a response**
Example: "What is it that makes this task so interesting for you?"

Clarifying questions **aim to elucidate**
Example: "Do you mean you are unsure about this task?"

Hypothetical questions **can produce creativity and a change of perspective**
Example: "If you could decide on the distribution of the work, how would you do this? How would you like things to be if there were no 'ifs' or 'buts'?"

In order to learn how to master your questioning technique, and with five or six questions get to the heart of a complex problem, you must start by experimenting. What happens to the conversation if you ask unproductive questions and then productive ones? Focus on how you could ask more constructive, and therefore more effective, questions. You can practice these skills in practically any situation, for example at a dinner party. Here are some examples of questions that progress the conversation:

"What do you really want?"

"What would you rather achieve?"

"What options do you feel are open to you?"

"What sort of help or support do you need in order to achieve your aim?"

"If you were guaranteed to succeed, what would you choose to do?"

"If success were guaranteed, how would you go about things?"

"How can you make progress, do you think?"

"What do you feel is the root cause of your problem?"

"How do you want to deal with this?"

"What do you need in order to be able to ...?"

"What is preventing you from ...?"

"What is missing in order for you to be able to ...?

"What is the deciding factor in your ...?"

"What is the next step?"

"When are you planning to ...?"

"Which of your options have you chosen?"

"What is the worst thing that can happen?"

"Say something more about that." (not a question, but ...)

"Do you have what you need?"

As I mentioned earlier, you should never think out your questions in advance. The questions are formulated based on what you hear the other person saying. You cannot pluck questions out of your head like taking them off a shelf. They must be based on the answers you get and what you find out when coaching.

Example:

Lisa: I'd like to clear out my garage.

Coach: What's preventing you from clearing out your garage?

Lisa: I never seem to be able to get round to it. I've been meaning to do it for years ...

Coach: What do you think you need so that you can do it?

Lisa: I don't know, maybe more time, I think.

Coach: OK, how could you make more time to clean out your garage?

Lisa: I just need to set aside some time to do it, I suppose.

Coach: How much time do you think you need to set aside?

Lisa: I think a few hours on a Saturday morning would be enough. Well, it's a starting-point at least.

Coach: What will you do?

Lisa: Well, I think I'll start this weekend.

Coach: You don't sound very sure.

Lisa: Yes, I'll start cleaning out my garage this weekend.

The best way of improving your ability to ask questions that will take the process forward, is to experiment and reflect on the different effects your questions produce, as well as ensuring you get frequent feedback on your dialogues.

Exercise 4

Ask a friend or colleague if you may coach them in some dilemma they have, using only the questions listed above. There is no need to ask the questions in the exact order in which they stand, but restrict yourself only to these.

Pay special attention to what you tend to do *instead of* asking these questions and listening to the answers – it will indicate the traps you tend to fall into.

In order to improve your skills, ask for specific feedback on how you ask your questions during a coaching conversation. Ask the person to be brutally honest so that you can recognise your tendencies and the traps you fall into. This is an important key to improving the quality of your dialogues.

HAVING EMPATHY

To be able to coach, you must to a great extent be able to enter into another person's perception of the world. The more you are able to acquire and understand the other person's perspective, the more effective you will become at communicating in different situations. What is required from you is that you are prepared to let go of the idea that your personal perspective on the world is the only true one, and accept the idea that people live in different worlds. This will lead to a better understanding of what people have to go through in order to take risks and face new challenges.

The following are some examples of the different worlds that we live in. Remember that anyone who believes in their own view of the world is usually also convinced that theirs is the only true picture of the world.

A coach who lacks empathy believes that their picture of the world is the only real one and may have thoughts like: "How hard can it be?" or "I don't understand why he can't get up in the morning – surely it's just a matter of deciding to do it ...?"

By developing your feelings of empathy, you will quickly be able to immerse yourself in the world the other person is living in and understand how it is restricting them. Only then will you be able to conduct a conversation in which you can meet this person on their own terms, and provide the tools to enable them to expand their horizons.

TRADITIONAL ISSUE-BASED COACHING

"You'll always be disappointed."

"It's dangerous to take risks."

"The world is full of obstacles."

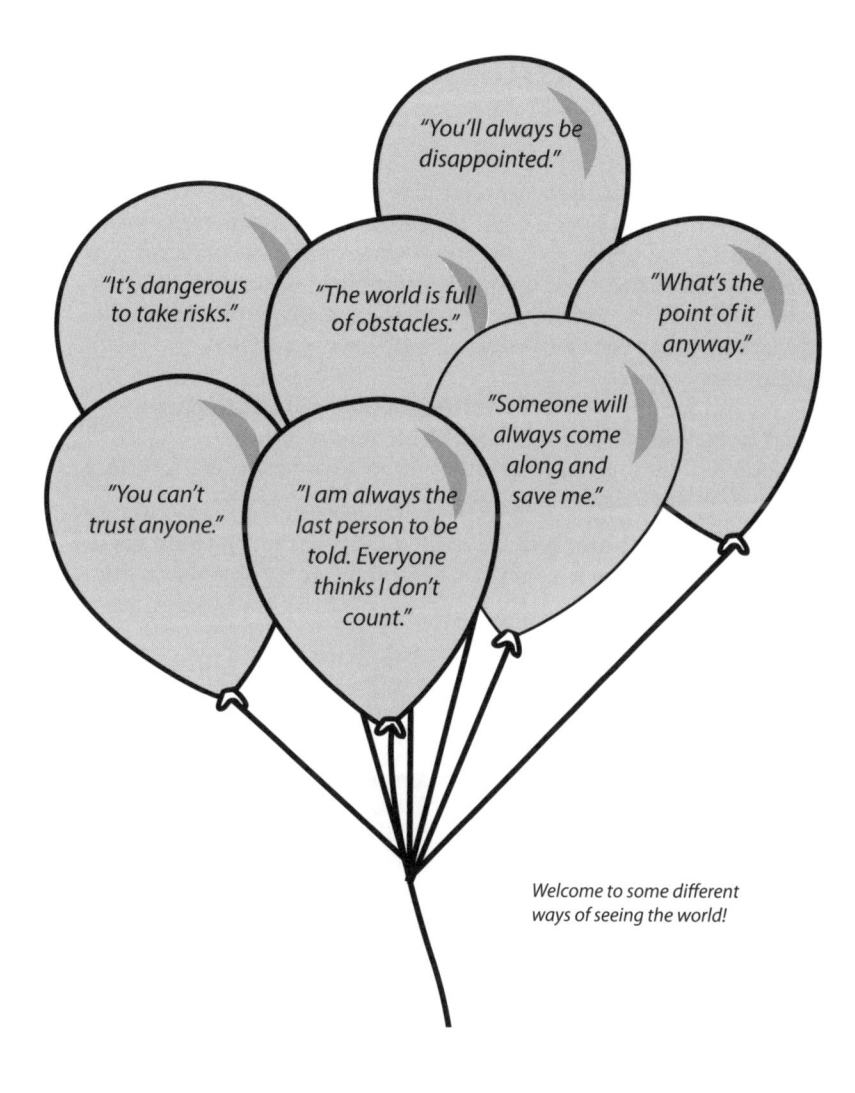

"What's the point of it anyway."

"You can't trust anyone."

"I am always the last person to be told. Everyone thinks I don't count."

"Someone will always come along and save me."

Welcome to some different ways of seeing the world!

Challenge the jobseeker's view of the world, for example by asking: "Suppose that your world is not real ... what would this mean for you?" But at the same time be aware that it can be frightening to accept the reality of other world views.

THEIR GOAL IS YOUR ASSIGNMENT

An absolute prerequisite in order to be able to coach someone is that there is a specific and defined goal. This goal is your assignment. Without it, you have no role to play. Never offer your services as a coach without having a specific mandate. It is your responsibility as a coach to ensure that the goal is clearly defined and clarified, expressed and established. Do not assume that your jobseekers already have a specified goal, as in nine cases out of ten *they don't*.

The criteria for any goal are that they should be specific, measurable and time limited. It should then be obvious whether the goal has been fulfilled or not – there should be no room for interpretation. Some examples of such goals are:

> "I will have a full-time job as a child minder within the local government children's daycare services, before the end of this year at the latest."

> "Within four weeks I will have decided on the 10-year career strategy which I am going to commit myself to."

> "Within three months, I will have a job as a programmer at Ericsson."

Many people feel annoyed at being forced into being specific, especially regarding the time aspect. Establishing a time goal carries the obvious risk of failure. It is much easier to state an unspecified time frame, such as: "just as soon as possible …". However, a fluid goal does not contribute to or support the coaching process.

> **It is your responsibility as a coach to ensure that the goal is clearly defined and clarified, expressed and established.**

There may be a lot of resistance from individuals, and the process of formulating an acceptable goal may be time-consuming and difficult. However, it is essential for the dialogue to continue. This subject is discussed further in Section 3.

TRAPS IN ISSUE-BASED COACHING

The most common trap relates to the point just made above, that as a coach you assume that there is an implicit goal. An example may be: "these people are unemployed, therefore their main aim must be to find a job".

One obvious trap is that without a specific goal you try to coach towards an unspecified variety of goals, back and forth. Your dialogue becomes unfocused and does not lead anywhere. You see so many coaching opportunities, and areas to focus on, that your coaching is "all over the place".

Once the goal has been defined, there is a further important observation to make – does the person own it? Another trap for you as a coach could lie in your simply taking at face value the jobseeker's claim to have a goal. This is not good enough. You need to check and confirm with the jobseeker that they actually 'own' their goal, that they firmly believe in it and are striving towards it. Reflect on whether the person can be believed when they say that they have a goal. If they do not sound convincing, then they are not owning their goal. Tell them so directly. For example, say: "You've defined a goal, but I think it sounds as if you're not totally committed to it. What do you say to that?"

The purpose of having a clearly expressed goal 'on the table' is to expose the real underlying situation and give the jobseeker a chance to identify a goal which they can wholeheartedly commit to. Only once this has been accomplished can you continue coaching.

However, lack of clarity over the goal of your coaching is only one of many possible traps you can fall into, albeit an important one. Further examples are set out below:

Possible traps in the coaching dialogue

- You are playing a role rather than being yourself.

- You are unable to establish a rapport/relationship with the person you are coaching.

- You can't stay silent.

- You keep offering advice, tips and solutions.

- You have a hidden agenda.

- You don't intervene but get bogged down in talk that isn't leading anywhere.
- You are locked in your own head, not out there in the conversation.
- You interpret what you hear.
- You act like an official, rather than being empathic.
- You are excessively empathic, almost like a therapist.
- You are the one with all the energy – you are the one doing the work and driving the conversation.
- You focus on your own performance, feeling that you must deliver.
- You want to cheer the other person up and don't allow them to be as they are.
- You are coaching without the person having an explicit goal.
- You don't listen enough.
- You listen too much.
- You are not present.
- You talk too much.
- You pile too many questions upon each other.
- You use questions that are too long.

Remember, do not get frustrated with yourself if you fall into these traps over and over again – it is all part of your development.

DEVELOPING YOUR BASIC SKILLS

Your training as a coach will be most effective when you focus on your 'traps'. This part is also the most difficult and painful. Of course you can reflect on what you have already mastered and celebrate that for a while before throwing yourself back into tackling those things you could do better. Many of my trainee coaches find themselves paralysed by feelings of incompetence, a mindset which makes them feel that they are absolutely useless at conducting a meaningful coaching dialogue.

At least half of your training is about becoming aware of the elements of coaching that you already do well, and those which you need to work on. In this way, you get a picture of your overall competence as a coach. Your competence revolves around two primary coaching skills:

- your ability to listen
- your ability to ask pertinent questions which take the conversation forward.

LISTENING SKILLS

To improve your listening, you need to identify those of your skills that you need to develop. Put into words the way you listen. It may sound like this: "I am more interested in delivering my own solutions than in listening to what is being said"; "I don't listen to the end of the sentence"; or "The other person doesn't really feel heard and understood when I am listening".

The more you become aware of your 'Achilles heels', the more effectively you will be able to work on them.

An example of how to start this process may be trying to explore your own attitude to listening. How do the following statement sound to you? *It is more powerful to listen than to speak. It is possible to save time and be more effective by listening. Listening is a prerequisite for achieving results. It is extremely valuable, rewarding and indeed crucial to listen.*

Be sincere and truthful when you answer the following question: "Do you subscribe to this view and does your coaching reflect it?" If you are not sure, then to become a good coach you have to work more on your own attitude to listening.

There is only one effective starting-point if you want to improve your listening skills, and that is to say to yourself: "I don't listen!"

In practice, when it comes to your ability to listen, you start training by finding out from your own environment. Ask those people around you, such as your close colleagues, your family, and your best friends. Tell them to be completely honest and specific in their responses. This approach may result in answers such as: "You don't listen when you are under stress" or "Sometimes you only pretend to listen." This is the kind of feedback which is invaluable in order to identify your present skill level.

> It is more powerful to listen than to speak. It is possible to save time and be more effective by listening. Listening is a prerequisite for achieving results. It is extremely valuable, rewarding and indeed crucial to listen.

You cannot possibly coach another person if you have not yet developed your own listening skills. In the method I teach it is even more important, since the coaching happens at a deeper level than the conversation itself. It starts from the expectation that the person who is being coached has one or more unproductive attitudes which are preventing them from achieving positive results. As a coach, you must then be able to deal with the person's whole way of being. See Section 4 for a more in-depth description of the skills required to be able to listen at a deeper level during a conversation.

QUESTIONING SKILLS

To be able to improve your skills at asking questions that will lead to progress, you need to be aware of your present skill at asking questions.

Exercise 5

Try a role play with someone who is skilled at dialogues. Ask for their feedback with a focus just on your questioning. The two central issues that you want to clarify are: "Can I ask questions at all?" and "How good are the questions I ask?"

Rate your questions on the following scale, with 1 representing the poorest response and 4 the best:
1. I only get monosyllabic and useless answers.
2. I get valid answers but I seem to be doing most of the work.
3. I get full and comprehensive answers, and the person opposite me is engaged.
4. The other person is thinking and reflecting, and is clearly working hard on formulating their answers.

Based on the feedback you get from this exercise, you should be able to identify one or more traps in the way you are asking questions. It may be that they are too long and complicated; that you don't wait for an answer; that you are thinking about your next question before you have heard the response to your previous one; that you don't listen to the answer so you don´t know what to ask next; that you don't really ask questions, you just tell the person what they should do (i.e. you are giving advice); and so on. These are just a few examples, but you may well identify others.

Once you have become aware of the quality of your questioning skills, you can identify what you need to work on.

We have now gone through the basic skills needed for jobseeker coaching. These are the basic skills which, once you have mastered them, will provide you with the starting-point for conducting productive dialogues, which will in turn lead to results. However, before you start having a productive coaching dialogue, you have to ensure that the basic preconditions have been met. We will look more closely at these in the next section.

SECTION 3
THE BASIC PRECONDITIONS FOR COACHING

CREATE THE PRECONDITIONS FOR COACHING

Government programmes, through a government Job Centre and other jobseeker initiatives, do not usually offer the basic conditions for coaching in the same way as when a person contacts a career coach themselves. In the former, the participants have not actively asked for coaching. They may expect to just be assigned to a post or to be given 'help' to find a job, with it being open to interpretation what kind of 'help' this might be. On top of that, conditions may be complicated by the previous experience the person has of government initiatives, which may not have been successful and may therefore have led to scepticism about what the process can offer.

The basic preconditions for coaching are:

- the jobseeker sees the benefit in being coached
- the jobseeker has confidence in their coach
- the jobseeker understands what coaching involves, and its purpose
- the jobseeker's goal is to find a job
- the jobseeker really wants to be coached
- the dialogue feels comfortable.

All these requirements must be met for coaching to take place. So I want to be quite clear and say: do not coach if the necessary preconditions cannot be met!

> **Do not coach if the necessary preconditions cannot be met!**

How many of the jobseekers you coach meet the above requirements? If your answer is 'almost none', then there is great potential for you to achieve markedly better results for the jobseeker. If your answer is 'almost all', then you are on track for the right preconditions for successful coaching.

Does the jobseeker have an unhelpful attitude towards you as their coach? Then you can be almost certain that the conditions for starting to coach are not good.

Jobseekers may be reserved, arrogant, resigned, sarcastic, confrontational, sceptical, blasé or non-committal. If good conditions do not exist for coaching, then rather than giving up, you should *start creating them*.

If you are working hard at this, you will already have gained both in terms of saving time and achieving a result, even before the coaching starts. That is because many of the obstacles before starting to coach are the same as those which are preventing the jobseekers from making progress when it comes to finding a job. In the following pages I describe how you can create the necessary preconditions for effective job coaching.

CLARIFY THE VALUE OF JOB COACHING

It is your job as a coach to 'sell' the value of job coaching. The only value of any interest to a jobseeker is to substantially improve their chances of finding a job, and you must be able to convince them that they can improve their chances, and more quickly, with a jobseeker coach.

This means that you must stand by your claim that your coaching is valuable and will clearly contribute to a better outcome. Ask yourself, hand on heart: "Can you do this?" If you have any doubts, then you must focus in on what is missing. This is something that you yourself must work on. What do you need to do?

A comparison: a jobseeker must be able to convince an employer that they are worth employing, otherwise there is no point in going out looking for a job. In the same way, you need to instil confidence that your coaching can produce results – if not, why should the jobseekers trust you?

In this respect, you find yourself in the role of a salesperson! Ask yourself – can you accept a person saying "No, thanks" and respect their position? If it feels alright for you that people say "No" then you will get even more who say "Yes". It depends on your own attitude. With a 'free' attitude, you create an atmosphere without any obligations, which is not about compelling but focused on creating opportunity. At the same time you show that you stand by the value of what you are offering: "I have something valuable to offer, *take it or leave it*, the choice is yours!"

You cannot control what people will feel and think about that, but you can show that you are prepared to stand by what you have to offer.

In practice, you need to discuss outcomes before you talk about how the coaching will work. Why? Because nobody listens to how the coaching process works until they have become interested in what they might get out of it. It might go like this:

Coach: Are you interested in increasing your chances of getting a job?

Jobseeker: Yes, definitely!

Coach: Good, because that is what effective coaching can do for you.

Jobseeker: How does it work?

Coach: Coaching involves ...

In principle, you should not explain anything about the coaching process until the other person asks to know about it.

DEAL WITH LACK OF CONFIDENCE

Lack of confidence can be due to you acting in a way that makes the jobseeker doubt whether they can trust you. It can also be that you belong to a professional group that the jobseeker has had bad experiences of in the past.

So it may have something to do with you, or it may not. The only way to find out is to ask and, as I mentioned earlier, to need to be able to cope with the response. Here are some examples of jobseekers' attitudes:

"I don't think you seem to know what you are talking about!"

"You Job Centre workers are all the same, you don't really care about me."

"If you can't fix me up with a job, then what are you good for?"

As the coach, it is vital that you do not feel provoked by such responses, but that you stay calm and accept the jobseeker's view of the matter. Just because they express themselves in this way does not mean that all is lost. Without becoming argumentative or confrontational, you should gently ask, for example:

"So you have doubts about my competence?"

"It sounds to me as if you don't have much confidence in our organisation?"

"So, what you want me to do is to find you a job?"

What you need to do is mirror the jobseeker's take on the situation, so that everything is clear and out in the open. Once the lack of trust is on the table, you must if possible try to win back their confidence. You can do this partly by listening to the jobseeker and accepting their position, and partly by trying to find out what is lacking, and what needs to be done in order to win his trust.

The usual mistake that coaches make is in thinking that trust is a matter of time. This is not true. Confidence, or lack of it, is created instantaneously as a result of how well you have been able to integrate the five basic coaching attitudes into your approach and behaviour. If these are integrated into you, you will win confidence. People will feel that you are empowering them and are on their side.

If the jobseeker appears not to trust you, some relevant responses may be:

"I am happy to tell you more about my professional background. What in particular is it about my skills as a coach that you are doubtful of?"

"What is it about me that makes you hesitate?"

If instead it is the organisation you work for that the person does not trust, you could for example say:

"I hear that you have been disappointed with our organisation up until now. Is it possible for you to give us/me a second chance?"

"I understand that you have had negative experiences in the past, and I'm really sorry to hear that. But can you consider the possibility that you might get some useful coaching/support here?"

"I hear what you are saying about wanting me to fix you up with a job but I also think that you realise that no-one can get a job for another person. What do *you* think?"

The conclusion of this part of the dialogue should be that you will have established a sufficient amount of trust between yourselves (even if it is not a huge amount) and that the jobseeker will be ready to commit to the coaching process (Your jobseeker may feel exposed but it really is worth it).

"So even if you don't have a great amount of confidence in either me or my organisation, do you feel confident enough to continue?"

CLARIFY THE PURPOSE OF THE COACHING AND WHAT IT INVOLVES

What is the aim of you meeting? If the jobseeker is not in agreement with the aim of your meetings, then you must make the purpose clear. The purpose is to increase the jobseeker's opportunities to find a new job. The goal is always to get a job.

Is the goal relevant for the jobseeker? If not, why not? This needs to be clarified. There may be many reasons why the jobseeker does not agree on the goal, and these reasons need to be brought out into the open.

Your challenge as a coach is to be able to accept a situation, even if the jobseeker is querying the purpose of the exercise (which to you is self-evident). Possible reasons for them being unclear about the purpose of coaching is that they are uncertain of the value of it ("What's in it for me?") or it could be that they are open to the idea of coaching, but do not have enough trust in you as their coach. Another reason may be that they are unsure whether their goal right at the moment is really to get a job.

The only goal which is compatible with the purpose of job coaching is that the jobseeker secures a job. If this is also the jobseeker's goal, you can go ahead with your coaching sessions. However, if it is not their aim to get a job, there are two possible options:

1. Invite and engage the jobseeker in the possibilities of finding a job.
2. Discontinue your coaching. If the jobseeker really does not want to find work, there is no basis for coaching. (Read the next section on genuine and false "No"s.)

What does coaching involve, and what does it mean to be coached? The answer to this question is of course crucial for a person to want to embark on the coaching process. "What am I getting myself into?" can be a question asked which may stir up many different emotions.

I recommend that you give a simple, brief explanation. Do not complicate things by elaborating on the complete history and methodology of coaching. I usually say:

> "I have expertise in coaching jobseekers. I can support through clarifying your goals, identifying any barriers in your way and giving you frank and honest feedback. Through the coaching conversation you will dramatically increase your chances of finding a job. You have responsibility for your job search, in other words it will be you who do all the work. My responsibility as your coach is to provide such good

coaching that your chances of getting a job will noticeably improve. Sometimes it can be a drag being coached: you will get some challenging questions and frank feedback. Coaching is hard work, but it's worth it because you'll be able to achieve a much better outcome."

Having explained what coaching is, for example according to the template above, it can be good to ask your jobseeker to relate back to you in their own words their understanding of what coaching is all about, so that you hear what has or has not sunk in.

CLARIFY THAT THE AIM IS TO FIND WORK

Most unemployed people want to work. However, there are many who, for different reasons, do not *seem* to want to work. They may no longer believe that this is possible. They may have ended up in a life on welfare benefits which has become more of a reality for them than a regular working life. They may have had a disagreement with the Job Centre and be more intent on battling it out with them. They have forgotten their original intentions.

My experience, after having worked with thousands of jobseekers, is that behind this state of powerlessness lies a will to take back the initiative and once more make a contribution to the world of work. However, after years of passivity, this may be deeply buried.

Then there are of course some people who have accepted the consequences of being unsuccessful in finding a job and have assumed responsibility in another way by saying farewell to a working life. I am primarily thinking of people over 60 who one way or another have made alternative arrangements to see themselves through to retirement – people who actually feel as if their working life is over. I therefore distinguish between two different attitudes to working, which I call a genuine "No" and a false "No".

Genuine "No"s

A genuine "No" relates to those who have taken responsibility for saying "No" to work. The most obvious characteristic of this group is that there is no trace of a 'victim mentality' when they talk about their decision.

It is best to let such people get on with their lives in whichever way they choose. Do not start an argument as to why they should go out looking for work, it just won't happen because that's not their agenda. Let them be.

False "No"s

This is a "No" based on resignation. A working life has become something unimaginable for people who give a false "No". They seem to have forgotten about, or abandoned, their goal of finding work. A false "No" may sound like this:

> "You know as well as I do that there are no jobs like that available. It's useless."
>
> "Let's see how it goes, eh? Things might get better later on."

In this case it is your job as a coach to clarify whether a "No" is genuine or false. If it is real, all you need to do is to end your coaching. But if it is false, you should start digging deeper to find out what the jobseeker *really* wants. A good question is:

> "Let's leave aside all the barriers for a moment. Let's forget all the 'ifs' and 'buts'. If there were no 'ifs' and 'buts', would you then want to find a job?"

To this question, 98% of the people who have given a false "No" respond with a "Yes". In such cases you just need to continue with:

> "So you actually *would* like to work. It feels impossible for you at the moment but I understand it's what *you* really want, am I right?"

Now you have a commitment to finding a job and you can build on this as the coaching proceeds.

CONFIRM WILLINGNESS TO BE COACHED

Willingness to be coached comes as a consequence of (a) being able to see the value in coaching, (b) feeling safe in the coaching process and (c) having a new job as the ultimate goal.

It is your responsibility to ensure that these three conditions apply to the jobseeker before you go ahead with your coaching sessions. If you have any doubts, you need to check that you have understood the jobseeker correctly by saying, for example:

> "So what I'm picking up is that you see the value in coaching, which is that you can improve your chances on the job market. What I'm also picking up is that you're committed to finding a job, and that you have listened to my explanation of how the coaching process

works. To me it sounds as if you are ready to proceed with me as your coach? Is that right?"

ENSURE THE DIALOGUE IS COMFORTABLE

The dialogue between you and the jobseeker needs to feel reasonably comfortable and natural. You should be able to talk adult to adult, without a hierarchical relationship.

If you feel uncomfortable, you have to do something about this. Ask yourself: "What is it about the other person or the situation that makes me feel uncomfortable when we are talking?" Once you have clarified what it is about, the next step is to ask questions of the person you are talking with. For example:

> "I get the impression that you want to get out of here as soon as possible ...?"

> "It feels to me as if you perhaps still have some questions about the coaching process, is that right?"

> "I get the feeling that you really don't want to be here ...?"

As coach, it is you who has to take responsibility for the relationship and atmosphere between you and the jobseeker and ensure that it is conducive to a coaching dialogue.

HEALTH PROBLEMS AND OVERARCHING PERSONAL PROBLEMS

Many coaches deal with aspects of rehabilitation, because health related issues are very common. Of course the health problems may be physical but they may also – often unconsciously – become psychological barriers. The same is true of other problems we come up against, problems which can sometimes feel overwhelming.

ILL HEALTH

Coaches often have to deal with jobseekers who are experiencing physical and/or mental problems which are limiting them. This can be a physical illness, exhaustion or psychological issues, amongst other things.

The question that arises is whether one should coach these jobseekers, in particular because coaching involves direct and honest feedback. My personal opinion is if the individual is expected to be able to manage a job on the regular job market, then jobseeker coaching is absolutely relevant. However, if the jobseeker is not expected to be able to handle a mainstream post, it is uncertain whether jobseeker coaching is suitable.

The best person to decide this is the jobseeker themselves, through asking questions. Such questions may be:

> "Do you feel that despite your health issues you are ready to look for a new job and start working?"

> "Are you able to take responsibility for your health being good enough to start searching for a job?"

The answers you get contain a lot of useful information. You may get confirmation from your jobseeker that they are prepared to take full responsibility for their health issues and start looking for a job. However, you may also detect that they are using their problems as a way of avoiding responsibility, when they say for example: "I don't really know how long my health will hold up ... maybe I'm not fit for work." Your response might be, "No, there is no way of knowing, is there? But is it what you *want*?"

A jobseeker may develop back pain whenever the pressure is on and it becomes hard work, using their back problem as a way out. This must be considered as unwillingness to take responsibility. Note that the point is not that the jobseeker should make one particular choice over another but that they *take responsibility for the decision they make:* "I am well enough to look for a job" or "I am not really up to looking for a new job."

Some jobseekers will find it uncomfortable to commit to a decision in these circumstances. It is much less demanding to sit on the fence, but it is also quite impossible to make any progress from this position. It may sound something like this:

"I don't feel well, I don't think I can cope with this ..."

Your answer might be:

"You are the only person who can judge whether that's the case. Only you can decide whether you are able to take responsibility for finding a job. If not, you need think about what you want to do instead."

Or:

"It sounds to me as if you are using your medical condition as an excuse to avoid taking responsibility for your job search. What do you think?"

Note the difference between taking responsibility – "Yes, I still have problems with my back, but I would like to try anyway" – and not taking responsibility – "I don't know, maybe I am not strong enough."

By the conclusion of this conversation the jobseeker must have decided whether they want coaching or not. Only then will there be a clear remit for you as the coach, which will increase the chances of achieving a positive outcome.

OVERARCHING PERSONAL PROBLEMS

Jobseekers may have other major problems which stand in the way of them actively participating in their job search, such as: financial problems; separation, divorce or bereavement; and alcohol or drug related problems (which can also be viewed as health problems). In these cases, it is essential that jobseekers deal with the overarching problem first; anything else would be inappropriate. The important thing is how they deal with, and take responsibility for, the overarching issue. It is also important that you respect the fact that every individual is unique and functions in their own way. One person who is in the middle of a divorce may be perfectly capable of looking for a job at the same time, while another may find it unthinkable. Examples of questions you might ask are:

"How are you dealing with your financial situation?"

"What do you need to do to be able to deal with ...?"

In regard to alcohol and drugs, it is not so much the substance use in itself that is the problem as the jobseeker´s *attitude to it*. Someone who has a drug problem may habitually try to hide it, and it is their attitude which may tip you off. You will usually find a mass of question marks around a person with a drug problem, and it is just this uncertainty that works against them when they are looking for a job. An example of a question you might ask is:

"I have no idea, but I feel I have to ask ... do you have a problem with drink or drugs?"

When the overarching problem, whatever it might be, is brought out into the open, it is up to the jobseeker themselves to decide how it should be dealt with, and what help they need. Frankly, you may not be able to offer any practical help in their current situation but you may be able to support the person to find other ways of resolving their situation. The jobseeker coaching should be postponed until the jobseeker is ready for it.

REHABILITATION

It may not be appropriate to engage in jobseeker coaching in its full sense when working with jobseekers who have a disability or impairment, but it is absolutely alright to let the dialogue be inspired by the coaching approach. People with various disabilities do not want to be seen as helpless. My experience is that those working with people with disabilities are well able to decide how and in what situations they (the worker) can use the coaching approach.

CONCLUDING WORDS ABOUT CREATING CONDITIONS CONDUCIVE TO COACHING

Make sure you do a final check before starting the job coaching process. If you want, use the following questions as your checklist:

- Does this jobseeker understand the purpose and value of job coaching?
- Do they feel confident having you as their coach?
- Do they agree with what the coaching involves?
- Are they aware that they are responsible for doing all the work?
- Are they prepared to set explicit goals for their job search?
- Do they take responsibility for their job search?
- Do they agree that this is the right thing for them to do right now, taking into account the state of their health etc.?

If the answer to each question is "Yes", then you can proceed and start talking about finding a job. If there are still a few "No"s, continue working on creating the necessary preconditions for job coaching.

Remember! Do not give up and label the jobseeker as hopeless, which is an easy trap to fall into. For a skilled coach there is no such thing as a hopeless case! Frankly, if you often feel that you are coaching 'hopeless' jobseekers, ask yourself honestly if you are in the right job? If your answer is "Yes", there is only one solution – get down to intensive training!

Does it feel like this section has a lot of 'ifs', 'buts' and 'maybes' before the coaching has even started? Yes, I agree, there are many things to consider, but if you are an experienced coach and are trained in listening beyond actual words, you will be able to detect what is going on without having to check each point one by one during your conversation, and will be able to focus on what is relevant. Let the headings in this section be your internal checklist, and use them when you are listening. It may take one or two discussions before you can fulfil the requirements of coaching, but this initial stage is essential, otherwise you won't have laid the groundwork for the coaching.

And the coaching process has actually already begun!

Even when the jobseeker has agreed to be coached, they may still of course retain unhelpful attitudes, such as 'let's wait and see', avoiding engagement in the conversation, being sceptical about your coaching, acting as if they have been forced to come and see you, being passive during the conversation, having unrealistic expectations and/or just looking for advice, help and solutions. Make sure you pick up on any such unhelpful attitudes in the dialogue as soon as you hear them.

In this section we have taken a closer look at the basic preconditions for coaching. The next section concentrates on explaining some techniques that really produce results – giving the jobseeker an opportunity to change their outlook from an unproductive to a productive one.

SECTION 4
ATTITUDE-BASED COACHING

FOCUS ON UNPRODUCTIVE ATTITUDES

The focus on a person's attitude is what makes this coaching method so unique. It may seem a little hard to grasp at first, but if you are prepared to spend some time focusing on this part of my book, you will be rewarded by improving the outcomes achieved by your coaching.

The purpose of all coaching is to give the person you are coaching new insights, which in turn gives rise to new actions, new ways of doing things, enabling the person tap into their energy and power or discover new opportunities to solve their problems.

So coaching aims to enable the jobseeker to draw on their strength and turn it into concrete outcomes. Another way of saying 'to coach' is 'to empower'.

Different people may vary in how productive their attitude is when it comes to the goal they are trying to achieve. By 'attitude' I mean here 'mindset', 'outlook' or 'way of being'. If a person has an unproductive attitude then it will hinder them from achieving their goal, while a productive attitude will increase their chances of getting the outcome they want.

There is no need to comment any further on productive attitudes here; when these prevail, people are perfectly capable of making progress through their own efforts. It is the unproductive attitudes that you, the coach, need to train yourself to listen out for. In order to be able to coach effectively in this way, you have to train yourself to listen for the person's attitude.

Practically speaking, it is about focusing on an unproductive attitude in the jobseeker, an attitude that is preventing the person concerned from achieving their aim. Once this unproductive attitude is identified, the jobseeker recognises how it can hold them back, which then allows them the opportunity to choose a more productive approach.

Note that I am not being judgmental in my use of 'unproductive' – it is not 'bad' or 'wrong'. I only mean that it is unhelpful in relation to achieving the outcome one wants.

Here are a few examples to illustrate what I mean:

Example 1 *Objective:* **Finding a spouse or partner**
Behaviour: Meeting potential partners but unable to decide; perhaps outwardly projecting an attitude of being aloof and cold, afraid, unworthy, critical or condescending.

Possible unproductive attitudes: Fear of being tied down, of losing their freedom and independence; feeling that there is a better match who they have just not met yet; "What if there is something even better out there?"

Example 2   *Objective:* **Improving your financial situation**
Behaviour: Always in the red at the end of the month; extravagant without having the money in the back to cover it; lots of small precarious loans etc.; debts continually growing as the person's income never covers their spending.
Possible unproductive attitudes: Behaving like an ostrich – burying their head in the sand; "I'm hopeless at arithmetic"; perhaps counting on parents to step in and cover it; finding it difficult to take responsibility.

Example 3   *Objective:* **Getting a job**
Behaviour: Unable to give a believable answer to the question: "Why should we employ you?" without starting to ramble.
Possible unproductive attitudes: Not seeing themselves or their abilities as valuable to a potential employer.

Example 4   *Objective:* **Getting a job**
Behaviour: Won't stop talking; expanding on every detail; taking over the interview; talking the potential employer to death.
Possible unproductive attitudes: "I know best"; "I'm a phoney, but if I keep talking maybe nobody will realise."

Example 5   *Objective:* **Being a good boss**
Behaviour: Talking a lot; making all the decisions; telling others what to do.
Possible unproductive attitudes: "I am the only one who knows how it should be done"; not having much regard for other people's abilities.
These examples may seem somewhat exaggerated but are plausible nonetheless. We tend to be blind to our own peculiarities and habits, and often we ourselves do not understand what is preventing us from achieving our objectives.

The bottom line is that if a person has not achieved their goals, this is probably because of an underlying unproductive attitude. This attitude may be more obvious to a coach or someone outside the situation than to the person themselves.
The coach's job is to skilfully surface the unproductive attitude which is preventing the jobseeker from succeeding in their objective. If you, as

their coach, provide the right feedback, the person becomes aware of their unproductive attitude and has the ability to opt to change it. A shift in attitude can happen very quickly and, once it has happened, whole different outcomes are within reach. You could say that the coach gives the jobseeker the opportunity to choose to change their viewpoint. What is needed is that the person themselves realises that they have something to gain from changing their attitude.

Sometimes it can even be effective to explore more closely with the jobseeker what they gain as opposed to what they lose by retaining their unproductive attitude. In most cases, people are not aware of how much their unhelpful mindset costs them, nor what they actually gain by holding on to it. To put it bluntly, the cost is often huge in terms of for example self-esteem, happiness, energy, health and life in general, while the gain is often about the avoidance of risks or of taking responsibility for their lives and their current situation.

For example, take the unproductive attitude: "I have too poor an educational background to be able to get an interesting job". Here, the cost to the jobseeker of holding that statement as true is that they do not apply for any jobs at all, or do not apply for the right jobs, and in turn all this costs them in terms of their happiness, self-respect, health and so on. At the same time, the gain in seeing it as true is that they avoid taking the risk of applying for the jobs they really want in order to, avoid the risk of being disappointed or, quite simply, avoid taking responsibility for their situation. Once it has been made clear how large the costs are compared with the gains, the incentive for them to change their attitude becomes stronger.

Remember that attitudes are *not* the same as the personal characteristics or qualities that the person has. Attitudes are more a question of outlook, a frame of mind, a 'way of being', how you look upon the world. This is something we choose either consciously or, more often, unconsciously, and it is something that can be changed.

If we work from the theory that the outcome we get depends on the attitude we have, then that means that we can achieve entirely different outcomes with different attitudes. A coach who masters this way of coaching can expect great results in a short time.

The first thing we have to train ourselves in is to hear the unproductive attitude, and you do that by learning to listen on levels other than just what is said.

LISTEN AT NEW LEVELS

To be really effective in the coaching dialogue, you have to develop the skill to listen not just to what is said but also to what is not said, on two levels other than what is actually spoken. We could describe it as there being three levels to listen on.

At level 1, you are listening to *what your jobseeker is saying*, the words they use. At this level we are usually talking about issues, for example how to get a job.

At level 2, you listen for *who the person is.* Specifically, what you want to be able to hear is if the person has an unproductive attitude which is standing in the way of them finding a job. You are listening for states of mind, feelings (such as anger, agitation, happiness) and mood or behaviour (such as dejection, confrontation, listlessness, nervousness etc.). It is about how this person *is* right now, their attitudes, outlooks and mindset.

You could describe it as the particular state of mind explaining a way of being, which in turn indicates an unproductive attitude.

At level 3, you are listening to find out the jobseeker's *intention*. What does this person seem to *want*? What lies behind what they are saying, why are they saying this at this particular moment? It may be that they want to

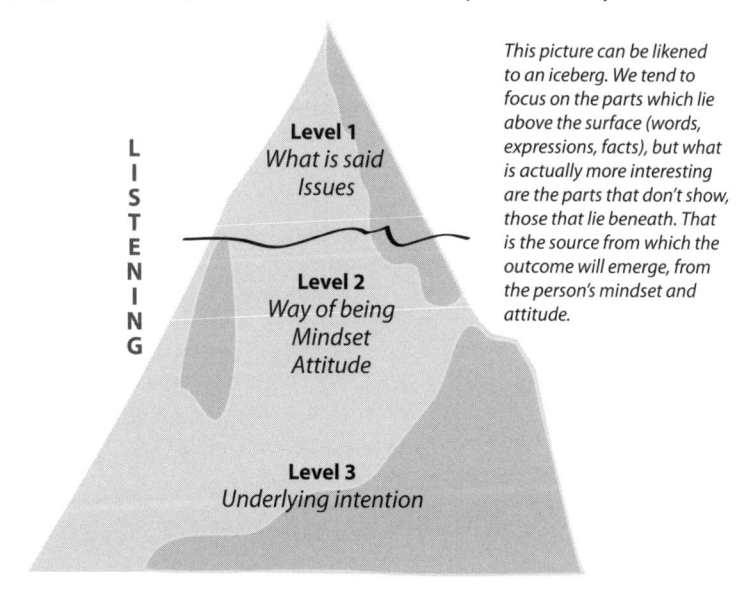

LISTENING

Level 1
What is said
Issues

Level 2
Way of being
Mindset
Attitude

Level 3
Underlying intention

This picture can be likened to an iceberg. We tend to focus on the parts which lie above the surface (words, expressions, facts), but what is actually more interesting are the parts that don't show, those that lie beneath. That is the source from which the outcome will emerge, from the person's mindset and attitude.

be heard or be consoled, or that they want to bring about change and so on. What kind of engagement is there?

The aim is to become skilled at listening on all levels at the same time and to pick up what is relevant in order to conduct a productive dialogue, a dialogue which takes the discussion forward.

LISTEN FOR WHO THE PERSON IS

When you have become better at listening overall, it is now about learning to listen at the level of attitudes.

When you listen at this level, you should try to set aside the words that the person is actually using. It is about disregarding what they are saying and listening for *who they are*. Start by asking yourself: how does this person appear to you. What unhelpful attitude/s do they have? Be prepared for this being unclear or abstract at first. The more you practise focusing on who a person is, the easier it will be for you to tune out the factual content.

What you have to do is stop censoring your perceptions of how you experience people in their environment, just become a little more blunt, but only in your own thoughts at first. You do not have to share your observations until you feel more confident using this method. What you do is go from broad, rather sweeping descriptions of how the person appears, to being more precise about how you perceive the person. Try to be as specific as possible – and as honest! Sometimes it results in a somewhat exaggerated, awkward description but it doesn't matter, just look on it as part of your training. In the following are some of the differences between general and specific descriptions of a person's attitude.

Broad description	Possible more pointed description	Broad description	Possible more pointed description
passive	dead, nobody home	compliant	scared to death
larger than life	arrogant, superior	blames others	irresponsible
inflexible	bigoted	hasty	doesn't listen, shuts off, doesn't give a damn
negative	a victim, a martyr		
laid back	couldn't care less		
evasive	glib, slippery, a sleazebag	chatterbox	self-centred, egotistical
		good-natured	a doormat
talkative	a know-it-all	always willing to help	a martyr, a saint
resigned	a victim		
restrained	sceptical	dominant	overbearing
careful	cowardly	critical	has given up
amenable	ingratiating, sycophantic, a yes-person	jocular	a buffoon
		insensitive	'Teflon-coated', shrugs everything off

Note that there is no intended 'equals' sign between these columns. The right column contains some *suggested* perceptions. There is a myriad of possible human behaviours and traits – your job is to pinpoint that person's type.

Note once again that the term 'unproductive' together with 'attitude' should not be interpreted as denoting 'wrong'. It is simply unproductive in relation to what the jobseeker wants to achieve. Suggested synonyms may be unfruitful, unhelpful and counterproductive.

LISTEN FOR THE UNDERLYING INTENTION

At this level you are trying to hear what your jobseeker's underlying intention is. What are they trying to achieve, what is their agenda? Quite often you *can't* put your finger on what it is exactly they want, and in such cases an appropriate coaching question may be:

"What is it you *really* want?"

"What is it that you want to achieve?"

"Do you want anything at all?"

"Why are you here?"

"What do you want the outcome of this conversation to be?"

Being absolutely clear about what the person you are coaching wants to achieve is a basic requirement for good coaching. The person you are coaching may not always be aware of what they want, and then it is your job to help them define this. Note that it is not what the person says but *where they stand* in the matter. It is all about what they want and how committed they are.

In some cases, you will uncover an intention that is not aligned with their goal. If the goal is to find a job, you may for example start to get the feeling that the jobseeker is uninterested in the conversation, does not seem to intend of making use of it. Then you can point it out: "You seem rather uninterested ..." Or it may appear as if the jobseeker is open to everything, but does not want to put in any of the work. Then you have to bring what you observe into the open: "You seem to be interested in everything, but it's as if you don't want to decide on one thing ...?"

Being able to listen at level 3 provides you with the key to why the person you are coaching is not making any progress. A basic presumption is that the person must want something, and here the jobseeker's attitude to what they want is revealed.

When you are training it is good to try to listen at one level at a time, in order to be able to start picking up what is going on at each and every level. However, when you are coaching, you are listening to all three levels at the same time, letting the dialogue be concentrated on where you detect an unproductive attitude.

When you have really started to hear and identify different unproductive attitudes and mindsets, it is now a question of how to deal with them. The next section shows how to proceed from here.

FRANK AND HONEST FEEDBACK

The crucial part of giving the person you are coaching the opportunity to change their unproductive attitude for a productive one is, through giving frank and honest feedback, making them aware of how it is their attitude that is preventing them from achieving their aim.

To begin with, it is important to emphasise that the starting-point for giving honest and candid feedback is the following:

- Relating to someone's potential involves starting from the assumption that people can cope with talking about difficult and problematic issues. And not just cope, but also learn something from the conversation when someone gives them open and honest feedback.

- The person offering the feedback must be crystal clear about their intention: and there is only one intention – to empower the other person!

When you coach at the 'attitude' level, you abandon the questions you use at the 'issue' level. Instead you point out something about the unproductive attitudes or frames of mind that you experience in the person you are coaching. If we return to the image of the iceberg, you are now coaching at level 2.

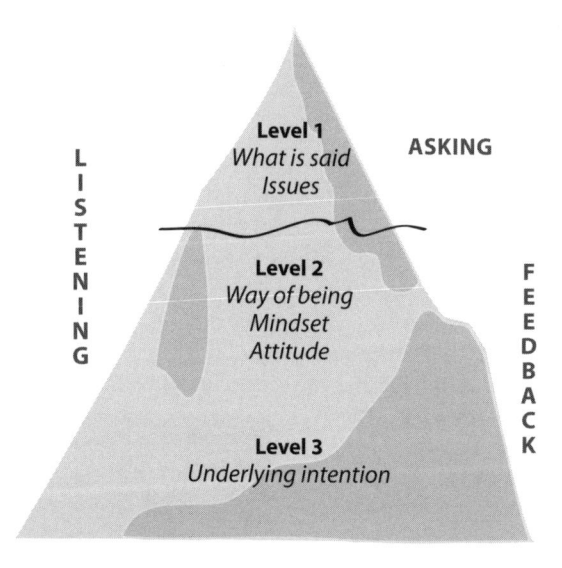

Level 1
What is said
Issues

ASKING

LISTENING

Level 2
Way of being
Mindset
Attitude

FEEDBACK

Level 3
Underlying intention

With open and honest feedback on the attitude, you give the person the opportunity to recognise their unproductive attitudes and so be able to choose to change them to more productive ones. Remember that attitudes are not the same as personal characteristics. It is not a question of a personality change. The person remains the same, but their approach has shifted from one way of being to another. And that will affect everything the person does, with the outcome being totally different. This concept can be illustrated by the following picture:

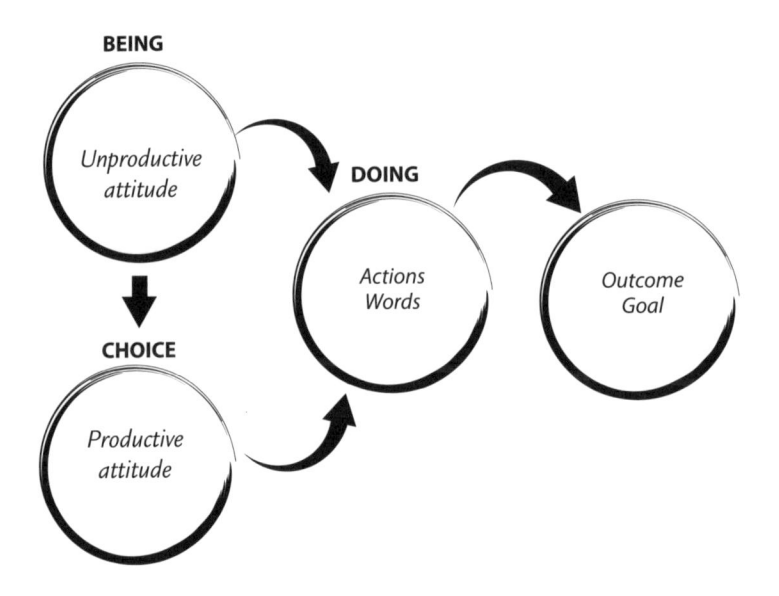

BEING

- Unproductive attitude

CHOICE

- Productive attitude

DOING

- Actions Words

- Outcome Goal

When an unproductive attitude is brough to the surface, then something tangible happens with the person or the dialogue. It is as if the jobseeker becomes a different person. The paradox is, however, that what is very obvious to a trained coach actually happens very subtly in the 'unsaid'. It could be described as something clicking with the jobseeker: 'clink', the penny drops, suddenly the insight is there. For the coach, it is about being extremely observant as to whether the 'clink' happens or not. It is the 'clink' that the coach is waiting for – this is what *should* happen as part of your coaching. It is the basis for the shift that involves changing from an unproductive attitude to a productive one.

> **'Clink' - the penny drops.**

I often get asked by trainee coaches, "But what should I do next? What do I do with the 'clink'?"

Actually, the answer is: nothing! It is the 'clink' you have been trying to reach. The only relevant intervention now is to make the jobseeker aware that the shift has happened, and the value of the shift. Have faith! Trust that the shift in itself will have a positive effect on the jobseeker's actions. Once the change has been consolidated, it *may* be the right time to start discussing the issue at hand.

The challenge for most of us when it comes to giving open and honest feedback is that we are too afraid of 'telling it how it is'. Often we do not admit even to ourselves that we are afraid, but instead dress it up as: "I don't want to hurt feelings or offend"; "I'm worried they'll fall apart"; or "I don't have the right to have opinions about anybody else".

Most of these reasons are because we want to avoid taking the risk involved in offering straightforward and honest feedback. We are just as interested in feeling comfortable and avoiding risks as anybody else, including those we coach. If you want to become skilled at coaching, you must work on your own fears, first by admitting that you are afraid, then by clarifying what it really is that you are afraid of, and then by challenging your fear – in other words, feeling the fear and diving in anyway.

What I mean by diving in is that, without it seeming the right moment, you decide to take the plunge and give your feedback, because unfortunately there is no such thing as the right moment to jump to the attitude level. There are no smooth transitions. These moments do *not* arise by themselves. You must just stop talking about issues, or the weather for that matter, and just dive in!

If you regularly have conversations with people for the purpose of supporting them, you should of course practice this in these conversations. Dive in, and dive in again! And again!

A STRUCTURE FOR FEEDBACK

To make it easier, there follows a structure for open and honest feedback, eight steps which you can follow while you are training. The steps are: 'diving in'; preparing the ground; defining the attitude; checking how the feedback is received; preparing for the effect; avoiding getting into issues; re-checking how the feedback has been received; and, finally, 'tidying up'. The feedback structure is a support, which means that there is no need to always go through all the steps.

'Diving in'
As mentioned, this means breaking from what you are talking about and starting to talk about what you want to talk about. Phrases that can help you introduce this can be, for example:

"You know what?"

"To be honest …"

Preparing the ground
Say clearly that you intend to talk about something which you think lies in the way of the other person's goal (for example, getting a job). Ask if they feel that this is all right to say it, i.e. make sure that you get 'a receipt' in the form of their permission.

"I'd like to talk to you about something which I think is holding you back from finding a job."

Defining the attitude

"To be honest, I am finding you really patronizing."

"You know what? You talk a lot, but *nothing* is happening."

"My comments slide off you. It's like talking to a Teflon pan."

Checking how the feedback is received. Did the penny drop? Did anything happen?
Even if you have given feedback, it does not mean that it has sunk in. Now you have to be observant to how the other person reacts to the feedback. If nothing happens, you can try repeating what you just said:

"I've just said that you don't listen! I said you don't listen."

"I've just told you that I feel you're confused, but you don't seem to have taken it in …"

"You're a windbag!"

If the feedback hits the mark, is taken on board and sinks in, you will notice that the jobseeker will change their demeanour. The arrogant jobseeker becomes lost, "… but what should I do instead?" The joker or wisecracker gets angry. It is a good sign that something has happened.

What makes it a little easier is that their attitude is present in the room with you. What you are trying to bring into the open is what is happening with the other person right here and now. You can say: "Now you're responding exactly as I've been trying to describe!" Give examples of how the person is coming over right at that moment.

Another way is to develop what you have just said. I have sometimes even gone so far as to play out a scene where I exaggerate the person's attitude, mirroring it back to them. (Of course not in any way with the intentioin of ridiculing them, only with the purpose of exposing something that is blocking them.)

Coach: I've just said that I feel that you are being very elusive, slippery, hard to pin down. I'm just skating around and I don't know how to take you. It's as if we're not really communicating. You're just dodging round me. Like a slippery eel. It's hard to have a proper conversation with you.

Jobseeker: But shouldn't we be talking about getting a job?

Coach: Now you are avoiding the subject again!

Preparing for the effect

Of course there will be repercussions from giving frank, honest feedback, and that is exactly the point. The effects are unpredictable and uncontrollable and therefore very scary for the coach. However, it is more frightening in the coach's imagination (in their horror scenario) than in reality.

What you need to train yourself in is the ability to take on emotional outbursts such as anger, tears or such like. The more you are prepared for it, the less you will experience it. I have coached thousands of people in this way, but on only a few occasions have I experienced great emotional storms in any way. Besides, even these have been justified and are not something you should avoid.

Another thing that can happen is that the person starts to defend themselves in one way or another. This is also a good sign, because it means that something is happening. A common trap in this situation is that you trigger your own defence mechanism and you start to argue with the person.

Avoiding getting into issues

Keep your dialogue at the level of *attitudes*! The person you are coaching often wants to get into discussing issues again, as this is risk-free and comfortable.

Coach: Alright, I hear what you are saying, but I don't want to talk about that. I want to talk about the way you *seem* ...

Re-checking how the feedback has been received
If your conversation has been 'eventful', make sure that you re-check what the jobseeker has taken from the discussion. Here it is about listening for whether they are feeling alright about the conversation. They may for example seem a bit subdued, which is perfectly natural and alright. It is important that you do not think that they must be cheerful after a coaching session. Being reflective can be much more productive than being upbeat.

'Tidying up'
If your feedback has not had any impact, and the jobseeker does not feel empowered by it, you may need to 'tidy up'. Start by listening to how they took your feedback and 'parrot' it. You need to take full responsibility for the fact that your feedback did not produce a result, and you do this by apologising for *how* it was delivered. It was the *'how'* that didn't create the intended effect of empowering the other person, and you have to take the responsibility for that. But you never need to take back what you said. It was what you perceived and is therefore valid for you. So only apologise for *how* you gave your feedback, not *that* you gave it, or *what* you said.

TRAPS IN ATTITUDE-BASED COACHING

Ask yourself during and after the coaching session: "Will my jobseeker be/has the individual been empowered by my coaching? Is the person showing any strength? Is there something that has shifted in the jobseeker's attitude? Can I expect something to come out of this conversation?"
If you are uncertain, ask yourself new questions: "What would empower this person? Appreciation? Structure? Candid feedback? Is there something I am holding back in the dialogue? What is missing in order for something to happen?"

This is where your coaching skills come in. Only you can decide if your conversation has changed anything for the future, whether there was any *empowerment*, whether you are on the right track and heading towards achieving the outcomes.

In most coaching conversations it is relevant to direct the dialogue towards the unproductive attitude; there is no occasion to keep to facts and issues all the time. In order to become a skilled coach, you must learn how to listen for any expressions of an unproductive attitude, and start talking about it.

The most common traps are where you remain at the level of talking about issues. Either you do not realise that you are still at that level, because you find it difficult distinguishing between the levels of issue and attitude, or you do not go deeper to the attitude level, because it feels uncomfortable for you.

The latter can manifest itself in waiting for a better opportunity in the conversation, a moment when you can give feedback, or hoping that the point you should be feeding back to your jobseeker will 'go away' and no longer be relevant to the moment. Even if you try, a possible trap may be that you try to 'package' it, try to deliver it so that it does not feel too 'brutal'. You are being too careful. The effect of this approach is usually that the person you are coaching does not get the message, and nothing happens.

Another trap is that instead of giving direct and honest feedback, you offer advice about how they should be. Instead of saying: "You know what, you seem to be stone cold dead!" you say: "You need to be a little bit more active."

A coaching dialogue is not a polite and agreeable conversation. The discussion does not have to be unpleasant but if you have a tendency to drift into 'politeness' or 'cosiness', then that is a stumbling-block that you have to work on. In most cases, this is about coming to terms with your wanting to be liked. As an effective coach, it is not your function to be liked. Your task is to empower someone else, and this is best done by telling it straight.

My usual prescription is, as usual, to practice! Learn how to separate issues from attitudes, and train yourself to 'dive in', down to the second coaching level.

DEVELOPING SKILLS IN ATTITUDE-BASED COACHING

As usual when you start to train, it is about finding out which traps you most commonly fall into, partly when it comes to listening for who the person is (under the surface) and partly when it is about giving feedback that empowers the other person.

Exercise 6
Think about a person you are coaching whom you are finding particularly difficult. It can be a person that you get a slightly uneasy feeling about as soon as you see that they have booked in for a session. When you are with this person you always get a premonition that the discussion is not going to lead anywhere. What unproductive attitude or way of being does this person have?

Exercise 7
Pick two TV show presenters that you know. Choose one you like and one you dislike. What attitude or way of being does the person you dislike have?

You are now training yourself to listening to the way of being rather than to comments, statements or actions. You can do this in any situation: on the bus, at home with your family, in front of the TV. What you want to acquire is the ability to be able to specify attitudes and ways of being.

Exercise 8
An efficient way to train is, after a coaching session, to reflect by asking yourself the question: "What unproductive attitude does this person have that is preventing them from achieving their aim?"

As you keep on training you will identify several different attitudes, some of which may be: passive, 'single-tracked', compliant, careless, lacking in initiative. Each and every one of these can be specified and defined even more, so that they hit the mark more accurately. Some suggestions:

Passive	uninterested, having a 'let's wait-and-see' attitude, lazy, indifferent, resigned, "dead"
'Single-tracked'	rigid, remote, unreceptive, stubborn, static, fanatical
Compliant	indecisive, vacillating, easily influenced, fickle, turns whichever way the wind is blowing, self-sacrificing, biddable
Careless	not hot on details, blasé, gives only 85 percent, cuts corners, unreliable, a fantasist with no handle on reality, slipshod, sloppy
Lacking in initiative	dejected, plays the victim, lazy, spoilt, paralysed, a jellyfish

When you get more specific in this way you notice that the first adjectives are quite neutral and tame. But deep down you are probably thinking rather of the other, more uncensored, words. These blunt adjectives can be extremely valuable to the jobseeker, so teach yourself to be concrete and uncensored. Ask yourself what you really think about the person you are coaching.

Exercise 9
Ask someone to practise coaching with you. Pick the worst attitude or manner that you can think of: aggressive, patronizing, confrontational, scatterbrained etc. Choose an attitude and ask your sparring partner to role-play a person with that attitude. You introduce your coaching session by saying: "How is it going with your job search?" The other person responds, trying to exhibit the difficult attitude or manner.

Your task is to give very clear feedback on this attitude as soon as possible. As soon as you have done that, you can end the exercise. Reflect on how it was for you. Were you impeded from giving your feedback and if so, why? Analyse what was holding you back. What did you do instead of giving feedback – for example, were you waiting for the right moment? Ask your partner for feedback on how straightforward and clear you were.

Exercise 10
If you want to intensify your training even further, look around you at your relationships with others and see if you have cause to raise something? The thing that is casting obstacles in your way as a coach is actually the same fear that makes you have unresolved issues with your nearest and dearest. So the more you challenge your fear, the better coaching skills you acquire. In all likelihood, you will get tangibly better relationships into the bargain. If not, you can assume that there is something about your way of being that is not empowering the other person. If this is the case, go back to the five points in Section I on the coaching approach.

SECTION 5
SOME COMMON CHALLENGES

MIXED ROLES – COACH AND GOVERNMENT EMPLOYEE

There are many frequently occurring challenges in coaching and it is easy to get caught up in them. Being prepared for how you as a coach can react to these challenges contributes to your coaching becoming more effective.

Many who are tasked with supporting job seekers are employed by local or central government and so have a parallel function, namely to ensure that rules are followed – for example the regulations relating to the payment of welfare benefits. A large obstacle to effective coaching is when the coach has a double function and does not clearly keep the two functions apart in their work, but acts in a way that blurs the boundaries.

One thing that can prevent the jobseeker from receiving effective coaching is that the official procedures become mixed up with the coaching. When you coach a person, you can never adopt the exercising of authority as a coaching method. Official processes and working with regulations must be totally distinct from the coaching dialogue. There are reasons for that.

Coaching is based on jobseekers themselves taking responsibility for their job search and having the right to find their own solutions. For that to happen, the person must feel complete confidence in their coach and feel that they, the jobseekers, have the power to steer their own job search. If the coach's position is restricted, for example because they resort to rules and regulations in order to get the jobseeker to do something, then the trust will disappear in the blink of an eye.

Example:
Perhaps the coach/Job Centre worker decides that the jobseeker is not showing enough initiative. Instead of using good coaching methods, the coach in this situation says:

> "But you know full well that you are obliged to apply for (x) number of jobs every week in order to qualify for unemployment benefits."

The very moment that the jobseeker coach expresses themselves in this way, they have completely negated the basic assumption that the jobseeker themselves should be able to bring about their own solution.

The exercising of authority has no place in the coaching discussion.

"Aha," any who have a double role will surely object, "so you mean we shouldn't follow the rules?" Of course you should. The authorities have their given remit to ensure that rules and regulations are followed, even though many current laws and directives are completely contrary to supporting people to take responsibility themselves for their future working life. Rules are rules and we are all bound to follow those that apply. The question is rather how you as a coach and employment official can exercise your official function without jeopardising the jobseeker's access to good coaching.

Start by being clear within yourself. Be aware of the damage that mixing the roles together can cause the jobseeker.

Because you know how valuable job coaching can be for the jobseeker's outcome, you can make it clear that getting the benefit of this support demands an investment which involves following the rules that exist. So you can lay it out as a choice that the jobseeker can make:

> "If you want coaching, which will probably increase your chances of getting a job, you have to make the decision to follow these rules. Is this of any interest to you? Do you want to agree to this?"

In this way, the employment officer/government official makes clear that the rules, and the following of them, gives you access to good coaching, which essentially increases the chances of finding work. In this way, the jobseekers themselves get to decide whether they want to follow the rules in order to enjoy the advantages involved. If they choose to have access to welfare benefits while also receiving coaching, then that is an adult-to-adult conversation. This is in contrast to an obstructive hierarchy which will not lead to anything good, where the jobseeker feels 'stricken down', like a victim of a process which they cannot get out of.

The choice not to follow the rules carries with it consequences, but who says that the jobseeker cannot consider the consequences? In order to be able to take responsibility for themselves, the individual needs to make that decision.

The next step is to clarify your role as coach and as government employee. It may sound like this:

> "I want us to concentrate our time and effort on your job search, and spend as little time as possible checking that the rulebook is obeyed. If I see that you're following the regulations, then I can be your coach. But if I start to doubt that you're following the rules, I'll have to put on my 'official hat' and sort it out. You will always know which role I'm in, and I'll never use my role as a government official during our

coaching sessions. My main interest is to coach you so that you can get what you want in life. That's why the best thing you can do is to take responsibility for managing this, so that I don't have to police you and 'nag'."

Even if your ambition is primarily to support the jobseeker in their job search, it is not certain that they will relate to you as someone who is supporting them. If they only relate to you as a representative of a public authority then there is *absolutely no basis* for coaching. In the first meeting you have to listen carefully for how the jobseeker views you and the coaching process. Statements such as: "I'm not really sure why I have to come here" and "You're supposed to check up on me, aren't you?" show perfectly clearly that the person is only seeing you as a government official. You also need to look out for any non-verbal signs of scepticism, such as a 'let's-wait-and-see' attitude or antipathy.

Never start coaching the jobseeker before you are absolutely certain that they are relating to you as their coach and support person. Otherwise, you are working against what it is you are trying to achieve.

SPECIFIC GOALS

Formulating a concrete objective when it comes to jobseeker coaching is easy: the objective is that the jobseeker finds a job.

Nevertheless, we are often careless when it comes to setting goals that really are goals. Most people have learned that an objective should be specific, measurable and time-limited. And, quite rightly, many jobseekers have a particular job as their goal, in other words the goal is definable and measurable. To be absolutely clear, however, the goal should also be defined in time – but that rarely happens in the case of a job search.

If you as coach ask the jobseeker *when* they plan to get a job, you are likely to hear them say that this is totally impossible to tell.

Of course, no one knows when it is going to happen, and this is not the point of a time-limited objective. Experience shows that a fixed-term goal has much more likelihood of being realised. All activities are driven by the goal and the deadline, which creates a whole different dynamic than if no time limit had been set.

ABOUT RESULTS, EFFECTIVENESS, AND WHEN WE GET STUCK

Your own idea of what effectiveness looks like, and how an outcome can be achieved, can stand in the way of your coaching being as empowering as it could be. Different people have different ways of managing projects and producing results.

What is your image of competence, capability, energy, engagement and driving force? A typical trap to fall into is that we often have a preconceived idea of how enterprising and capable a person can be and act. What does your image look like? If you are clear about how your own picture appears – and that this is *your* picture! – then you can also reduce any risk of that preconception hindering your effectiveness as a coach.

Different people create results in different ways. Some use their drive and are enormously energetic and 'on the go'. This is perhaps the most common image when we talk about capacity. However, there are other ways of producing a result. The outcome depends on *who you are* rather than *what you do*. So it can be a trap to coach someone with the aim of getting some action out of them, of getting them to engage in a whole mass of activities.

An outcome can be achieved, for example, by the person being astute and sensitive, in other words they understand on a deep level what people around them say and mean. These skills are absolutely central to salesmanship, for example which is geared to getting results.

To be reliable, and to have the ability to do what you have said you will do, is a quality which is the basis for all outcomes. So it can be more effective to have three activities/actions on one's 'to-do' list every week and really follow them through, than to try to do a whole lot of things at once.

Reliability can, in its turn, make a person instil a feeling of trust in others, which is an enormously valuable ability when it comes to getting a result. People who listen to this person rely on what they say.

When you are coaching, you need to listen for the result-oriented qualities your jobseeker has or does not have and adapt your coaching to the

> Abandon your preconceived image of what 'ability' looks like and be open to the fact that there are different ways of getting a result.

person before you. In summary, you need to give up your preconceived image of what 'ability' looks like and be open to the fact that there are different ways of getting a result.

There are also many ways of regarding 'effectiveness'. A national encyclopaedia defines 'effectiveness' as 'the relationship between the input into an activity and the resultant outcome of that activity', in other words the ratio between output and input.

Effectiveness is probably the most misconceived notion in trade and industry. The most common interpretation is that 'effective' equates with 'fast'.

My definition of effectiveness is 'to achieve what you intended; to reach the goal you want'. The journey, in other words the activity and input, does not have to be undertaken at breakneck speed.

Effectiveness can be to reflect on the most appropriate next step, i.e. what measures would make the greatest difference to an undertaking right at this moment.

Doing a little research before barging ahead can be another effective approach, even if it seems time-consuming. This may involve creating a really clear and specific picture of the job they want and look only for those appointments that fulfil the criteria - but with total commitment! - instead of going after everything that moves. Most jobseekers are looking for only *one* post and it is important that it is plausible and reasonably long-term. For some professional groups this means that there are very few jobs available, and if you want to go after them it is really important that you invest a great deal of time and effort in the process.

To stay calm, be patient and be able to accept a setback and keep going nevertheless, is another example of effectiveness.

So what does 'effective coaching' look like? Note that even the coaching part of the exercise should be evaluated and measured in the form of specific, measurable results otherwise it could easily become too abstract. A pitfall here is to measure it in terms of well-being, insights and personal health instead of cold, hard facts.

BEING STUCK

Are there people you coach with whom you fall into an unproductive series of meetings, where you both know how the meeting is going to turn out and where you both know that nothing will happen?

In this situation, as coach you need a fresh start. Probably there is also some feedback which you have withheld from the person you are coaching. You know for sure why you were not making any progress. What you have to do is interrupt the unhelpful routine that you have got yourself into. You could do that by saying, for example:

> "I don't think these meetings have been as productive as they could be for some time now and I take full responsibility for this. I have let them go on, knowing that you wouldn't get a result. But now it's time to call a halt. It's not right that we have meetings that aren't going anywhere. What do you think?"

But before you say this, you need to have dealt with the feedback that you have not yet delivered. You have to ask yourself: "Why isn't this person finding work? If I were an employer, why wouldn't I employ this person?" Then you will get the answer to what you need to say to the jobseeker.

The crucial thing about fresh starts, however, is to be able to put a stop to the unproductive element and start something new, which may be rather difficult because it was you yourself that got into a situation that was not making progress.

It is not uncommon to meet jobseekers who are a long way from doing any kind of job hunting and who are quite content with an existence subsidised by welfare benefits, an existence where regular work seems utopian, a fantasy. Such a person is putting all their focus on maintaining their current situation, organising it around their knowledge of the benefits system. This person puts very little effort, if any, into getting a new job. It is as if that kind of future is too vague. This is a natural development for someone who has been living on benefits year after year. That kind of existence becomes reality and the days slip by. You do not notice when two years or four years have passed. Anyone can end up in this situation.

I usually describe the phenomenon as the 'A-track' (working life, which has been forgotten and seems unreal) and the 'B-track' (life on benefits, which seems real and is what everything in life centres around). This individual has, without noticing it, come to organise their life on the B-track.

> **The A-track (working life) seems unreal.**
> **The B-track (life on benefits) becomes reality.**

The trap for the coach is to start judging, criticising and censuring. Indeed, according to most moral systems and accepted norms it is considered *wrong* to be living as someone on benefits does, but if you are to coach someone into work, it is not effective to start condemning.

The coaching task here is to have a *'wake-up discussion'*. This involves making the person aware of how their life is developing and explaining that they are in no way heading towards getting a job. In this way you can find out what the jobseeker *really* wants.

Example:

Coach: I've heard you describing how your life seems at the moment, and that you've been living on benefits for quite a while. What I'm wondering is how you see your situation in five years. What will it look like?

Jobseeker: Well, by then I'll have a job.

Coach: And how did you get this job?

Jobseeker: Well, you know, five years is a long time. I'm bound to have a job by then.

Coach: You know what? I have bad news for you. You are not on your way to finding a job!

Jobseeker: But how can you say that? You don't know that!

Coach: Nothing in your current life situation, or in what you're doing day by day, is leading to you having a job in five years' time. In fact, quite the opposite. And if you want to have a job in five years, then it's time to *wake up. Now! You are in no way heading towards getting a job*! And if you want to be, *then you have to wake up now*!

Jobseeker: You're making it sound melodramatic. I'm doing just fine.

Coach: Sure, you're managing for now and getting by on benefits. If you still want to be doing this in two, four or even five years' time, there's no reason at all to worry. But if you want to have a job in the future, your current situation *is dramatic*, that's why you need to wake up now and do something. You're not heading that way *at all*. So how do you want things to look in five years' time?

Jobseeker: Of course I would want to have a job by then.

Coach: That's why you need to wake up *now*.

Jobseeker: OK, I hear you. What do I need to do?

COMMON UNPRODUCTIVE ATTITUDES

"IT'S IMPOSSIBLE TO GET A JOB"

The decisive factor in any job search is the jobseeker's own attitude towards the possibilities.

The first basic requirement, if a person is to succeed in their job search, is that they consider it possible to get a job. However, many long-term unemployed people have long ago given up hope and become resigned, which is fully understandable given the circumstances. They have come to the conclusion that it is impossible to get a job. They have, you could say, parked in the 'Impossible' zone.

There are many excellent government programmes aimed at helping people find work, but they all fail to take into account this basic factor, i.e. the resignation felt by so many jobseekers. It is just not taken into consideration! And this leads to the steps in the programme being met with "I can't" and "It's no use". Time after time, job hunts break down because the jobseeker's whole attitude says that it is impossible, not because the job market is impossible.

In order to be able to successfully support the jobseeker in looking for work, a basic first step has to be taken, and that is that the jobseeker goes from seeing employment as impossible to believing that there is one job out there for them. If you do not succeed in getting the person to believe that, you can spare yourself from carrying on further: it will not lead to an outcome. As you know, this step is a huge part of what the whole coaching process is about. And it is not an easy step.

In practice, this means that you, by using your coaching skills, are offering your jobseeker the opportunity to get from a position of "there are no jobs, it's impossible" to that of "there may be one job for me". The important thing is that the jobseeker themselves chooses to accept that they have something to gain from changing their attitude, namely that *their likelihood of getting a job will increase dramatically*. Let us take a closer look at how you might lead the coaching discussion.

Impossible

As a jobseeker coach, you need to understand the background to why people have dug themselves into an attitude of 'Impossible'. Maintaining that something is impossible, and having given up, is often a way of justifying one's passivity, not having to take any sort of action. This is a safe position. You get out of having to take responsibility (allowing the role of victim to flourish!) and avoid taking risks.

It is often a mixture of both causes that lies behind this attitude. Choosing to accept that something is 'Possible' carries with it a risk of failure, and at the same time requires you to take more responsibility. It is, naturally, much more comfortable to stay in the 'Impossible' zone.

However, there are at least two different kinds of resignation. One of those truly has a quality of real hopelessness, sadness and desperation. There is no victim mentality involved here, only unhappiness. This kind of resignation needs to be responded to through the coach listening, listening and listening so that the person gets in touch with how desolate, downhearted and depressed they really are, until everything has been said and every emotion expressed. The occasional tear may fall, which is perfectly acceptable. The coach should not confront, just be there for them so that the jobseeker can pour out their distress.

Afterwards, it is usually possible to move on, but let the jobseeker take the initiative. It will happen if you just keep back and stay silent. Eventually you can make a pact to accept the dejection but not let it hinder the jobseeker in their job hunt. Then you give the jobseeker the opportunity to consider that there might be *one* job for them out there.

Another kind of resignation is a deliberate one, permeated with a victim mentality. "It's no use, there's no way, nobody wants me. I've applied for about 200 jobs already." Here it seems as if the jobseeker *wants it to be impossible* and is putting up a strong argument to support their theory. In this case, the person is more dug into their position than in the first case. In this situation, it doesn't help to listen, it will not lead anywhere. It is better to interrupt and confront them, show them that behaving like a victim and feeling sorry for themselves is preventing them from finding work. I will shortly say a bit more on how coaching can take someone from this position to one of 'Possible'.

However, a feeling of resignation may also be infused with bitterness and indignation at how things have been. In this case, the jobseeker needs to start by actively trying to put past history behind them, in order to be able to meet the future without being burdened by what has gone before. In the coaching conversation it can take the form of an endless retelling of, for example, unfair treatment in their previous job. The tale may very well be true, but the problem is how the jobseeker relates to it. In the worst cases, they may be looking for redress or revenge in relation to their previous employer, something which is often not possible to achieve. It only has a negative effect on new work plans and makes the person ineffective. Your task here, as their coach, is to support them, so that they can put the story of their ill treatment behind them. To make this possible, you first have to ask the person to consider that they have something to gain from doing this. If you get their consent, ask the jobseeker to reflect before your next meeting on everything they need to express and put into words in order to be able to put it all behind them. Explain also that your role during your next meeting will be to really listen to everything that needs to be said so that it can then be finished with. Point out that it is not a question of forgetting or repressing anything, only ensuring that it will not interfere with future actions. The agreement that you and the jobseeker reach is that they undertake to put their past behind them once everything they have to say has been said.

Possible

What is needed in order for someone to get a job is that they must think it is 'Possible'. To do this is to put themselves in a vulnerable, uncomfortable position, full of risks of failure and carrying with it the requirement to start taking responsibility for making something happen.

It is true that it can feel much more comfortable to be in the 'Impossible' zone, but this has the effect that the individual will not achieve an outcome, that nothing will happen. In the longer term, maybe over several years, this is a heavy cost to have to bear.

Your job is to explain these two positions, with all their pros and cons. From this clarification, it is up to the person you are coaching to make their choice. If the person chooses to maintain their standpoint that it is 'Impossible', there is nothing more for you to do together. No coaching in the world can help if someone chooses to park themselves in the 'Impossible' zone. Their first step must always be to consider that it is 'Possible'.

> **No coaching in the world can help if someone chooses to park in the 'Impossible' zone.**

When you convey this reasoning to the person you are coaching, it can be really helpful to draw two circles. From the illustration, you can talk about what the respective positions involve in relation to the desired outcome. For example: "Impossible – no work, but the person avoids risks and responsibility"; "Possible – the only position in which the person has a chance of getting a job, but it is at the same time risky and uncomfortable."

Impossible
Avoid risks
Avoid responsibilities

Consider Possible
Risky and uncomfortable

This is how some coaching dialogues that are wrestling with the problems of the 'Impossible' versus the 'Possible' may sound:

Example:

Coach: It sounds to me as if you see it as impossible …

Jobseeker: Are you kidding? Don't you read the newspapers, there just aren't any jobs. And anyway, nobody would want to employ someone who's been out of work for three years!

Coach: So, you see it as impossible?

Jobseeker: See it as? It *is* impossible.

Coach: OK, if you think it's impossible to get a job, then you and I have nothing more to talk about.

Jobseeker: What? But you're supposed to be helping me!

Coach: No, I'm not supposed to be helping you. I'm supposed to be supporting you to get a job you want. But if you don't think it's possible that you can get a job, then I can't do anything for you.

Jobseeker: Yeah, but they told me …

Coach: Whatever they told you, all job hunting starts with considering the possibility that you can get what you want. I totally respect your position if you can't consider that possibility, but in that case there is no job search.

Jobseeker: But I can't just start believing something because you want me to, can I?

Coach: I don't want anything. You decide for yourself what you want or don't want. And you don't even have to believe it's possible to get a job, you just have to *consider* that it's possible.

Example:

Jobseeker: ... but there just aren't any jobs! I've applied for 50 jobs. I didn't get any of them. It's no use.

Coach: Now, I'm going to say something. I'm telling you that the fact that you don't see it as possible that you'll get a job is a *bigger* obstacle to getting a job than the actual job offers. Let me say that again: the fact that you think getting a job is impossible is a bigger obstacle than the shortage of jobs! I totally understand that you feel that way, but I'm still telling you that this is the biggest obstacle between you and your new job.

The most important thing you can do in order to get an end result in a job search is to show the jobseeker what the deciding factor is in the ongoing task, namely how they regard the likelihood of finding a job. And unfortunately there is only one alternative in order to go forward. With an attitude of "it´s impossible", the outcome will be no job!

You can even have this discussion with a group of jobseekers. At the end of the discussion, you come to an understanding with the group: that the work put into looking for a job rests on the basis that we consider that there is a job for each and every one of us. If anyone does not see it that way, they should not take part in the exercise.

Also in individual coaching sessions, you need to come to an agreement with the jobseeker that the ongoing task rests on the basis that it is possible to achieve their goal. On this fundamental point the whole coaching process stands or falls, and it is important that both parties are in agreement with this.

"I CAN'T/DON'T WANT TO CHOOSE …"

When a person is faced with a choice and is, for example, undecided over two possible career paths or two possible job offers, it is easy for the coach to fall into a trap. A person who is undecided appeals to you to give advice, to tell them what the right choice is. Even if you are skilled enough not to make a choice for the person you are coaching, it is easy to end up in a 'plus-and-minus', 'pros and cons' discussion which is totally unproductive. Trying to coach an ambivalent person with 'plus-and-minus' lists is to start at the wrong end of the process. In other words, it is not the choice itself that is the problem. What is holding the person back is their *attitude* to having to make a choice in general.

Here are some examples of unproductive attitudes to a choice situation: "I must be sure that I'm making the right choice." The truth is that you can't. Making a choice always involves a certain amount of risk, and there is no such thing as a 'right choice'. "But what if I will change my mind tomorrow?" "What if something better turns up?" This makes you wonder how long this person should actually wait, and behind this unproductive attitude lies the truth that they simply do not want their own decisions to prevail. Or they are afraid of their illusory freedom being restricted. The usual 'gain' with such attitudes is the avoidance of risk.

> I must be sure I'm making the right decision.

> What if I change my mind tomorrow?

> What if something better turns up?

You therefore have to steer clear of the choice itself (the issue) and target this person's attitude towards making choices. What does it look like? Mirror it!

"I'M NOT GOOD ENOUGH"

Not having enough self-esteem to feel you have any value in the job market is a common attitude, which is of course a great drawback and can have many forms of expression. As I have said above, a good indicator of this attitude is what the answer is to the question: "Would you want to employ yourself?" If the person finds it difficult to answer "yes" to this question, then their self-esteem is low.

How then can you work with low self-esteem? You might think it obvious that years of having a poor self image cannot be fixed with a wave of the hand. However, it is possible to change a person's perception of themselves and their ability, provided that the person sees that there is something to be gained from it. If someone sees lack of aptitude as their greatest drawback, it is in principle always the case that other people have a different and more positive opinion about the aptitude of the person concerned. Your job is to give the jobseeker the opportunity to change their perception of themselves and their competence, and take the stance that they have something to contribute.

First of all you have to clarify that the barrier is the jobseeker's negative perception of their worth and therefore their competence, and that this image is purely subjective and untrue. Here you can set the jobseeker the task of finding out how they really behave, how others regard them and their ability. You simply tell them to interview people around them. When the jobseeker can process and recognise what it is they can contribute, and what the good things about them are over and above their actual competence, then they will also be able to stand by that. The jobseeker adopts the position that they have something valuable to offer. If they start having doubts again, support them to return to that position.

Example:

Coach: So you don't feel that you can offer an employer anything?

Jobseeker: No, my skills are really out of date. I don't even think that I can remember as much as I should, in order to be good enough for a job.

Coach: Can you consider the notion that you have something of value to offer an employer?

Jobseeker: No, that's pretty doubtful …

Coach: So you have nothing to offer that an employer can use?

Jobseeker: Well, maybe I'm good at talking to customers.

Coach: So, your feeling for customers and customer relations is something you're good at?

Jobseeker: Yes, I'd say so.

Coach: Do you think this skill is valuable enough for an employer to want to hire you?

Jobseeker: Well, maybe in the right type of work.

Coach: OK, can I count on you to stand by your acknowledgement that you have a valuable skill, which is to be able to talk to and deal with customers?

Jobseeker: Well, I suppose so …

Coach: "Suppose"?

Jobseeker: Yes, I stand by my acknowledgement that I have that skill.

Coach: Great.

As a jobseeker coach you will certainly have situations of this kind, which vary in their degree of difficulty. Those that you find hardest and feel inadequate in are of course those which you need to develop yourself most in.

Most job searches include getting a few "No"s before you get the longed-for positive reply from an employer. It is easy to feel downhearted and dejected on getting a "No". It is also easy to take a "No" personally, taking it to mean "I'm not good enough" or "I'm never going to get a job".

Train your jobseekers to cope with "No". The great secret is namely that the better we are at coping with "No", the better our chances of getting a "Yes".

How do you train them? I usually say that, statistically speaking, people need to apply for an average of 39 jobs in order to get *one*. Whether that is true or not is irrelevant. As a jobseeker you can use the statistics positively by deliberately collecting "No"s. Stick a piece of paper on your fridge door, with 39 squares on it for putting crosses in, one by one. "Hurray, another 'No'! Only 24 to go!" Then you will have truly changed your attitude to "No"s, in this case to the rejections you get from your applications.

Another way of dealing with this is to view "No" as a shower of rain. You cannot take personally the fact that it is raining. When it is raining "No"s, that doesn't mean that the individual is worthless or that they are never going to get a job. It is not personal, it is just a natural phenomenon, like rain.

This is a good topic for discussion with individual jobseekers who are afraid of failing or who find it difficult to take setbacks, or in a group as preparation for setbacks.

"BUT I'M 57 ..." AND OTHER BARRIERS

We all have mental barriers around the issue of 'why nobody wants to employ *me*'. It may be because we are the wrong age, we do not have enough education and training, we have the wrong skills, too little experience, too many children, the wrong ethnic background or whatever.

> **And once again: the disadvantage is never the real barrier!**

Barriers may be general, such as lack of job vacancies in a certain part of the country, or personal obstacles, such as being too old.

I maintain most emphatically that the disadvantage is never the real barrier when it comes to looking for a job. Yes, that is what I said: *the disadvantage is never the real barrier!*

No, the problem occurs when the jobseeker is convinced that the obstacle is real, that it really *isn't* possible to find work when you are 55 years old. Everything they then do and say, and everything that happens, will be aligned with this 'truth'. So if you apply for a job with the conviction that your 'problem' will make it impossible to succeed, then you will not achieve an outcome. "Everyone knows that you can't get a job once you're 50."

Of course, a person has every right to see things in this way, to buy into this truth. However, with this attitude, an unnecessary consequence follows: no job! An alternative attitude, which leads to a quite different result, is: "maybe there is *one* job out there for me, even though I'm 56". This attitude has a chance of leading to a quite different outcome compared to the former example.

An important question is how you yourself regard barriers in a person's circumstances. Some jobseeker coaches have themselves fallen into the attitude that some barriers are real. So, hand on heart, are there some obstacles which you yourself have bought into and see as real? Then you need to change your own attitude, because it is standing in the way of good coaching. One firmly held 'truth', for example, is that it is almost impossible to get a job if you have the "wrong" ethnic background.

Agreeing that it is impossible does not help the jobseeker with the 'wrong' background. Nor does it help if you deny the fact that it is much more difficult. A question that reflects a coaching attitude may be:

"If we can now agree that it's more difficult for you, how are you going to deal with this, given that your aim is to get a job?"

> How is it that two 57-year old jobseekers with totally different attitudes to their 'age barrier' get quite different results in their job search?

A basic precondition in order for you to go on coaching where there are barriers is, as before, that you can accept and be totally comfortable with the fact that the person you are coaching has this deep-seated attitude to the barriers. The fact is that the person has every right to go on thinking that the problem is making it impossible for them to get a job. That is their choice and their decision. Your job is to spell out to them that:

> *The perception that there is a barrier is a bigger obstacle than the barrier itself.*

And when the jobseeker can see that their attitude to the barrier may not be the only possible attitude to have, then that gives them the opportunity to change their attitude to a more productive one.

Jobseeker: But you just can't get a job if you are over 50. I know because I've applied for more than 40 jobs now.

Coach: Yes, I really do understand your frustration over not having got what you wanted. But equally I know that if you choose to believe that nobody over 50 can get a job, then your attitude will ensure that your next 40 applications will be rejected too. Would you be able to at least consider the possibility that there is *one* job out there for an ancient 52-year-old like you?

So for the coach, it is about homing in on, and bringing out into the open, the relationship that the jobseeker has to their disadvantage, finding out if they are being held back by their perception of their disadvantage and give them the opportunity to choose a different attitude.

SECTION 6
SOME TOOLS

TOOLS FOR MANAGING A JOB SEARCH

There are many common challenges which arise in jobseeker coaching which are easy to get stuck on. Being prepared for how you can approach these challenges will contribute to the effectiveness of your coaching. Below I set out some tools which can be useful in driving forward a job search.

YOUR PURPOSE IN LIFE IS YOUR STARTING-POINT

Most of us have chosen a profession based on the current job market ("I just fell into this career path"; "dad and granddad were both lawyers"; "it was just assumed that I would take over the company/estate"; "I thought I was interested in the natural sciences" etc.) without ever having reflected on anything as abstract as the meaning of life, your purpose in life, your mission (vocation, calling), how you want to express yourself, or whatever you want to call it. In the past few years there have been several books on the topic of the meaning of life, such as *The Soul´s Code* by James Hillman and *The Alchemist* by Paulo Coelho. This is not surprising. In my work, I meet many successful professionals who, despite claiming to have the dream job, do not feel satisfied or fulfilled. It is as if life 'lacks purpose'.

The reason, I believe, is that historically it has not been usual to associate work with pleasure. It simply has not been relevant to ask yourself: "What am I really passionate about?" or "What is it I love doing?" Historically the issue of being able to support yourself has carried much more

> "In the end it is the seed we carry within us which gives our life its meaning, without which our life is wasted."
> CG Jung

> "Pluto called it daimon, the Romans talked of man's genius. Today we use words like spirit and soul."
> James Hillman

> "Even before reason has taken form, our inner being struggles against its truth."
> Plotinos

weight than it does today. Now our primary needs are to a large extent taken care of, and so more existential questions emerge, including those that relate to our working life.

To start in all seriousness from our life's ambition when we start to look for a job is often a totally new experience for most, and can at first feel abstract and strange. "How will I get a job this way? I can't even find work at all so how can I afford myself the luxury of getting the job I really love?" But it is a much more sustainable foundation for building a professional life than the reasons I mentioned above. To clarify our ultimate purpose in life, and work from there, even increases our chances of finding work because, amongst other things, we summon up more enthusiasm, something that shines through in the recruitment process.

It is important to point out that each individual naturally decides for themselves how much weight they give to this as a starting-point. Some have a great need to do it, others less so; some know what they want, others do not. Some think that the reasoning is too hard to grasp. Whichever argument you hear when you are coaching, accept it and let the individual develop it in their own way. Or, if there is a great deal of resistance to the idea from the beginning, do not get into a discussion.

To coach someone in the direction of a life purpose is not a simple task. You need to have experience yourself of how tricky this can be to formulate. I recommend that you seek coaching yourself and work on your own life purpose before you start to coach someone else in it.

In practice we have to work on formulating what our life purpose might be, by addressing ourselves to a lot of questions. This then forms the basis of the ongoing job search. The process takes between 3 to 6 weeks to work through, with the help of coaching, and is a good investment of time and effort. It is like doing research.

Examples of exploratory questions:

- Which work tasks do you like best of all in your present/previous job/s? List them!

- For each one, what is it about them that makes you enjoy them? What's that one 'thing' about them? Be as specific as you can.

- Which situations – stages of work, contacts, contexts, activities – do you feel best in? Why?

- What kind of work task could you do without – either now or in the past? What is it those tasks are missing?

- Looking back, which workplaces did you enjoy best? What were they like? What were you doing that you enjoyed?
- In which moments of your working life have you felt most fulfilled and content?
- What is it in (x) occupation that is so fun? What's the one thing about it that made it good? Go into one particular job or task that the jobseeker has chosen.
- If you could contribute one unique thing to the world, what would it be?

The answers to these questions can help you pick out the 'golden thread', discern who this person is, find one core theme which you can use to guide the person forward towards a relevant definitive statement of their objective or purpose in life.

The following are examples of definitive statements which can be used as a 'map and compass' or as a business concept in the task of finding work. Use the statements in order to match them to job advertisements and concrete job offers. "Will I be able to contribute what I want to in this job?"

"If this is my purpose, how do I go on to find the right job for me?"

"My purpose is to bring clarity and order …"

"My purpose is to enable people to feel good …"

"My purpose is to construct something …"

"My purpose is to refine and improve …"

"My purpose is to support other people …"

"My purpose is to create aesthetic environments …"

BEING SPECIFIC AND SELECTIVE

There is a common misapprehension that the more people widen their job search the more chance they have of getting a job. I would claim that the opposite is the case – if you go after every job possible, you become less effective than if you are focused.

So a common stumbling-block for jobseekers is to 'keep all doors open'. It is a familiar unproductive attitude. 'Keeping all doors open' makes a person reluctant to go in any particular direction. "Here I am, keeping all doors open – and not a thing is happening!"

Experience shows that the more specifically and precisely a person defines their wishes in relation to what type of work, field of work, kind of workplace they want, the more effective that person will be in their hunt for a job. Narrowing down alternatives does not mean reducing your chances. On the contrary, the paradox is that your chances actually increase! There are three reasons for this:

1) A consistent and targeted action creates better results.
2) An action based on a strong aspiration influences a person's behaviour, for example at job interviews.
3) The jobseeker avoids becoming paralysed by too many options.

Here are two examples of how it may sound:

Employer: Why did you apply for this job?

Applicant: Well, I'm looking for anything at all, actually.

Employer: Why did you apply for this job?

Applicant 2: I really enjoy the kind of work the job involves.

Another common trap for jobseekers is being too flexible, not being discerning enough. This trap is about not paying enough attention to your own wishes. This is rooted in low self-esteem. Many competent people unnecessarily deny their own wishes and content themselves with something they frankly are not inspired by. This is how it can sound:

Jobseeker: Well, I would rather work in marketing, and would prefer to have responsibility for staff, but I can also work in a position with a little more autonomy, for example in product sales.

We can assume that this is a highly qualified person in the area of marketing, with several years' experience in leadership and management teams. There is no reason that this person should not follow their dream, at least in an early stage of their job search process. This tendency to sell out makes a person ineffective at looking for a job. The coach needs to coach the person in self-esteem. (Of course, there is also the opposite unproductive attitude, which is to be *too* selective, but that is not what I am talking about here.)

To be able to target those jobs that the jobseeker really wants, but also to be able to evaluate a job offer, it is good to have prepared a personal job specification in advance. This serves as both a map and compass, which can be used to reflect both the kind of work sought and any jobs that are eventually offered. With a job specification, you lay the groundwork for a solution which is as long-term as possible.

Examples of questions to be addressed in a job specification:
- What is the most important driving force for you?
- In what context do you want to make a contribution to that one thing you are most passionate about?
- What duties would you like your work to involve?
- What level do you want to work at?
- What is important for you in a workplace?
- Should the workplace be big or small? Private or public sector? A large company or a smaller one?
- How wide a geographical area are you prepared to consider?
- What is the minimum salary you'll accept?

When it comes to being specific, the most target-orientated job specification I have ever heard is this: 'I will become the tourist manager in my home area.'

JOB STRUCTURE

Some job seekers are more focused on the structure that their future employment should take and forget about the content. If they are too fixated on the structure, this can be an unproductive attitude. The reasoning is that if you dedicate yourself to the thing you are really enthusiastic about, you will be more content in the long run. It is therefore better to use the content of the job as a starting-point than to focus only on the structure. Here are some examples:

A secure full-time job becomes two part-time ones
A woman, 45 years old, living in a small town in which there were comparatively few job opportunities, was totally fixed on finding full-time permanent employment. When she became clear about what, for her, the work had to involve, she started looking for two part-time jobs which met all her demands in relation to the content of the work.

The structure gave way in favour of the content and she achieved a lifestyle she was happy with.

Freelance becomes salaried
A woman, 33-year-old, had been getting by for many years in a freelance capacity but had great difficulties getting business (it was hard to find customers). She was very fixed on the notion of being self-employed because it offered more freedom than being in regular employment. In reality, this freedom caused her to pay highly in terms of worry and of constantly having to work evenings and weekends, with few rewards and a life at subsistence level.

For her, just thinking about paid employment equated with thinking about imprisonment. But when she found a job which involved something that appealed to her, it was liberating for her to get a salary every month, to be able to go home at five o'clock every day and to stop worrying.

Search for permanent employment leads to self-employment
A man, aged 52, was employed as a gardener by a local council but was made redundant because of cutbacks. After some years on a fruitless search for a new permanent post, it occurred to him that the flowerbeds, trees and lawns were still there and that somebody had to take care of them.

He started up in business and offered the local council his services. A few years later, he also had contracts with neighbouring councils and had started employing people.

So be attentive to the jobseeker's attitude to the working structure they would like. Being altogether too rigid in regard to structure can be unproductive. If you sense that it is a major barrier in their job search, lay it out on the table. As usual, say what you are thinking:

> "This obsession with finding permanent employment ... I think it can be a barrier for you..."

> "Right, you are convinced about freelancing as a form of work, but what will it lead to really?!"

THE JOB APPLICATION

What the jobseeker has to offer, their 'CV', is usually set out in the job application form. It is of greatest importance that the form is effective and communicates what the jobseeker has to offer. Nevertheless, I meet an improbably high number of jobseekers who use very poor quality job applications.

You should go through your jobseekers' application forms and give straightforward and honest feedback until they are fit for purpose. If not, the consequence will be that the person will not be successful in getting interviews. If I meet a jobseeker who is motivated in their job search but has not had an interview for a long time, I know straight away that their application is not fit for purpose.

It is never the case that you should write the application for the person you are coaching, but you need to coach the jobseeker into producing a suitable application. I do not intend to deal with how to write an application in this book.

NETWORKS

More than half of all jobs, roughly, are arranged through personal contacts. You have to take this into consideration when someone is looking for work, and not just rely on job adverts.

An alternative way is to go through people you know. The jobseeker has much to gain from being able to communicate their plans for the future in as concrete terms as possible, in whatever situation they find themselves in. If, for example, a person meets people they know, their answer to the usual questions can be clear and concise. For example:

> "Fine thanks, I'm concentrating on finding a job in retail sales at the moment."

If instead the answer to the question "How are you?" is "Oh, fine" then the jobseeker will not get the effect they want from the personal connection.

It is important that you, as their coach, illustrate how networking actually works. Each person the jobseeker meets has in their immediate circle 40–80 people that the jobseeker does not know. When the jobseeker is specific about what they are looking for, there is a greater chance that a neighbour/friend/friend-of-a-friend will suddenly think of, for example, a brother-in-law who is the sales manager of a grocery business.

Note that this is not the same as asking acquaintances for help. Point out the difference between asking for help and being clear about your direction of travel, with the intention of helping those around you to make associations and find connections in their networks. Many will not be able to make connections at all, but someone will, sooner or later, when you are least expecting it. So the jobseeker needs to make it a habit to always answer concretely in a conversation with people around them.

Some jobseekers are embarrassed about being this explicit. Feelings of being unworthy restrict them and they think: "I mustn't disclose my plans" and "What if they don't work out?"

At the end of the day, this comes down to coaching the jobseeker to feel that they have something valuable to offer. Verbalise the fear. "What is the worst thing that people would think about you if you were to talk about your future plans?" "Can it be worth 'bragging' if it may actually lead to a job?"

Practise a role play with the jobseeker if they are resistant to being explicit. This resistance is blocking the whole job search, so it's a good investment of time and effort.

'Cold calling', i.e. ringing up a company and presenting yourself on the off-chance, is something that most people think of as terribly laborious. I have never recommended this to a jobseeker. There are very few people who give a good account of themselves in such conversations, and it rarely leads to a result.

BACKWARD PLANNING

Action plans have for a long time played a central role in the kind of support offered by employment offices and job centres. Planning is not wrong, but the importance of action planning should not be overstated. The jobseeker's association with the action plan that is devised is often weak, so it has little worth. Besides, people have different needs when managing a task: some feel supported by an action plan, while others feel it is irrelevant.

If the jobseeker wants to have an action plan for support, I recommend the principle of 'backward planning'. Backward planning starts with establishing a date by which the jobseeker will have their new job. Draw a simple timeline, with the present date at one end of the line and the date of the reply with the future job offer at the other end.

Example:
Now _____1st Dec

Now you start the task of planning backwards. How many interviews does your jobseeker need to go to in order to get a job? The person should judge this for themselves, based on the field of work, their place of residence etc. When you have discussed this together as far as you reasonably can, the person writes in the number of interviews on the timeline, weeks before the reply about the new job comes in.

Here is an example. Let us say that the jobseeker reckons that they need to go to 5 job interviews in order to get a job.

```
                    7 Oct   15 Oct   27 Oct   29 Oct   5 Nov
                    Int.    Int.     Int.     Int.     Int.
Present _____|_____|_____|_____|_____|_____1st Dec
```

How many jobs do they need to apply for, in order to get the chance of 5 interviews? In order to answer that, the person needs to think about how effective their applications are. Do their job applications lead to an interview in half or a third of the cases? Let us say one third. That means that the person has to apply for 15 jobs. Write in 15 application submission dates on the timeline.

```
                  August    | September    | October
Present _____1st Dec
               4 applications | 8 applications | 3 applications
```

The next step is that the person needs to find 15 jobs to apply for. When will they do this? Be definite and write the dates on the timeline! Is the time span reasonable, considering the backward planning that was done? Or does the timescale need to be adjusted, so that the person can 'own' it and take responsibility for it being realistic?

```
              July  | August | September | October  |
Present _____|_____|_____|_____|_____1st Dec
              Find   Find     Find        Find            = 1 job/week
              4 jobs 4 jobs   4 jobs      3 jobs
```

Planning backwards forces us to organise our efforts around a goal, rather than setting off from the present into an unknown future. Of course, even with backward planning the future is still uncertain; the difference is that you *approach* the future in a different, more productive way. The more a jobseeker can summon up a feeling of "this is how it's going to be", the greater chance there will be of getting that job.

BEFORE THE INTERVIEW

If the person you are coaching is on the point of going to one or more interviews, it is good to focus in on a few things.

The most important thing to remember before an interview is that it is a business meeting on equal terms. The applicant is there to see if they want to give 40 hours a week of their life to this workplace. The employer wants to meet the applicant to see if the person is someone they want to offer a job to.

> **It's a business meeting on equal terms!**

Unfortunately, there is sometimes a culture among both many employers and recruitment agencies that job applicants should be grateful for being considered for a job. This creates an imbalance in the dynamics in the recruitment process and the applicant can easily end up at a disadvantage. The job applicant can easily forget that they are also at the interview in order to see if the work meets *their* wishes or list of demands. It is easy to start 'proving your worth', showing that the 'burden of proof' is on your side, instead of showing what you have to offer.

It is often assumed that someone looking for a job is certain that they want the job at any price, when it should actually be a business discussion on equal terms where both parties size each other up. The key is to approach it with an attitude of "I have a valuable skill which I eventually might consider offering to this workplace for at least 40 hours per week", irrespective of how the other party behaves. Of course I do not mean that the person should overdo it and act in a supercilious manner, only that they remember their worth. In that way they also become a more attractive prospect to the employer.

Remember that the meeting is about the jobseeker being a resource that the employer may consider being interested in. The coach should listen for the jobseeker's attitude to interviews. If they have an unproductive attitude, as described above, then the coach needs to raise this in discussion, with the aim of changing their attitude.

The purpose of the interview for the jobseeker is to establish whether this post is for them and if it meets their most important requirements.

That is why it is important to have a clear job profile specification for the jobseeker. Even if they have been out of work for a long time, the next job should be one that feels right for them, one that the person can be content in. To just plod on thinking "I'll take anything" is not going to be sustainable in the long-term. The coach is fulfilling an important function here by laying things out and clarifying them.

It is good to practise interview questions with the jobseeker before the interview takes place. In this way you can spot any possible unproductive attitudes and give feedback. This will tangibly increase their chances. Of course, how much work you have to put in will vary from one jobseeker to another.

Go with your gut feelings. When you look at it from the employer's perspective, would you honestly and seriously consider hiring the person sitting opposite you? Only then should you let the jobseeker go to an interview. If you have the slightest doubts, you have to continue giving feedback on what it is that is causing you to have doubts.

Prepare the jobseeker for adapting to how the employer has set up the interview. Interviews may take different forms. Sometimes there are several people from the company present. The employer may do all the talking instead of asking the questions. A good metaphor is to imagine a dancing couple, with the interviewee as the female partner. As interviewee, you let the employer lead and you follow.

Perhaps the jobseeker has been to several interviews without success. In this case you both need to try once more to find out what is going on in interviews and what went wrong. Here is an example of feedback before an interview:

Example:

Coach: Now that you've been offered a job interview, I'm aware that there is something about you which, if I were an employer at the interview, would make me have doubts. Can we talk about it?

Jobseeker: Er ... what do you mean?

Coach: What I'm going to say now is intended to improve your chances of getting the job, nothing else. What I'm thinking about is your way of sometimes hesitate about what it is you really want, of being unsure and vague. This is what would make me doubtful about you.

Jobseeker: But sometimes I do feel unsure of myself and vague.

Coach: Yes, and that's understandable. What I'm talking about is that sometimes you sort of dissappear, you're not present. It's as if I can't be sure that you are still in the conversation. Do you see what I mean?

Jobseeker: Yes, yes I do. My children sometimes shout at me, "Mum, come out of your bubble!"

Coach: So you recognize yourself in my description?

Jobseeker: Yes.

Coach: How can you watch out for this habit when you're at a job interview?

Jobseeker: Oh, I know how to keep it in check. It's just a question of catching myself doing it ... I need to think about my children and the "bubble".

Coach: Can you do that?

Jobseeker: Yes, I can. And thanks for bringing it up.

A fundamental precondition for getting a job is that the jobseeker believes in themselves and their own ability. You can ask the question: "Would you employ yourself?"

If the jobseeker is hesitant in their answer, if they can't clearly answer "yes" to the question, then you need to practice more with the person so that they can take responsiblity for having something to offer an employer. Perhaps you both need to formulate exactly what the person's contribution to a workplace might be.

Engage the jobseeker in understanding how the work you are doing now will lead to them to being able to give an unequivocal "Yes" to the question as to whether they would employ themselves. What do they need in order for them to be able to say "yes". What can the person acknowledge they are good at?

A trap here can be that the coach buys into the jobseeker's view of themselves and their inadequate ability. The accepted remedy for this is to enhance their knowledge and skills. In certain cases this can be perfectly appropriate. But if the person has the attitude: "I am not good enough", they could get themselves a PhD and still not change how they regard their ability. In their own eyes, they are as just as 'not good enough' as before.

It is not until you can put yourself in the place of an employer, and can honestly and realistically imagine offering the person a job, that you can let them go to a real interview.

SECTION 7
SOME ILLUSTRATIVE EXAMPLES

COACHING IN PRACTICE – REAL CASES

Below are some examples aimed at illustrating what a change of attitude can achieve. Some of them were given to me by Job Centre workers who regularly use coaching in their contacts with jobseekers; some are my own examples; and others come from coaches who trained with me. Please note that the examples clearly illustrate that this method is not nearly as time-consuming as some people wrongly believe.

CHANGED HER ATTITUDE TO THE BARRIERS

A woman (58), who felt a little bitter and unsure and who had poor self-esteem, was trapped in her "I'm too old" attitude. In the coaching conversation, she decided to change her attitude in order to "seize the power" – her own expression! – and to start believing that she had something to offer. She rang up about a job she had applied for. The response was that they had already called to interview all those that they wanted to meet. But she did not give in and, based on her new attitude of 'seizing the power', she insisted that she "had plenty to offer". She was also offered an interview – and got the job.

TOOK A STAND FOR THE VALUE OF HER OWN CONTRIBUTION

A woman had met with her Job Centre worker off and on for the past few years. She had a dream of having her business as well as a knowledge of massage and reflexology. What she really wanted was to build that knowledge up into her own company, but she was stuck in the attitude: "there surely won't be enough customers, it'll never be profitable". She also did not have a licence/formal authorisation to practice. All the time she kept coming up with new excuses:

"The Job Centre will need to pay for my training."

"Employers won't give me contracts if I don't have a licence."

"I can't afford it right now. I'll need to stay on benefits a bit longer."

When she was given feedback on her unproductive attitude, that she was letting circumstances and barriers take over and was not accepting the fact that she was skilled, the penny dropped. Five days later, she came back to apply for business start-up grant.

> "And if I don't get a grant, I'll start up my own business anyway, because I can't keep going on and on like this any longer."

FROM IMPOSSIBLE TO CONSIDERING IT POSSIBLE

A computer programmer, originally from Iran, was totally dejected. He had applied for countless jobs as a programmer without having got any. His unproductive attitude was that he was completely stuck on the kind of job he wanted, namely as a programmer, preferably with the company that he had been made redundant from. When he realized that this attitude actually created a barrier, he was able to also start considering alternatives. When he started believing that he could at least get *some* kind of job, and began considering different fields of work, he got, through contacts, a post as a teacher of maths in an independent school for young people who were in trouble or at risk, a job he was very content with.

FINANCIAL PROBLEMS GOT IN THE WAY

A woman was meeting her employment officer for the first time. They had previously only communicated over the phone and by letter. It had not been pleasant, because it usually resulted in the 'official hat' being worn. She had, amongst other things, even had her benefit stopped.

When they finally met, the employment officer/coach wanted to know what she actually wanted from her job search. She said that she did not want a job at all, and was only interested in knowing what she needed to do to keep the benefit cheques coming. At this stage, it would have been easy for the coach to 'shut up shop' (which he should have done had he followed the rulebook).

Instead, he thought about the coaching 'way of being' and asked her what made her say that she did not want to work. She then explained that she had enormous debts and that no matter how much she worked she would never get above the breadline. Nor was she allowed to see her daughter because of some incident in her past. The coach did not give up but said:

"It sounds to me as if there are other things that are more important for you right now than looking for a job."

After talking it over a bit, they agreed that the woman would see a social counsellor before she planned her job search. There she would hopefully get some help with debt management.

This example illustrates how, when there are overarching problems, then they need to be dealt with first.

FOUND HIS OWN ANSWER

A young man, who was a programmer and had graduated two years before but had no work experience, came to the Job Centre for a discussion.

"I've applied for everything without getting a response. I don't see what more I can do."

He was complaining, and with his very first sentence he shifted responsibility over to the coach. After the coach had asked if he wanted coaching, the whole discussion was about shifting the responsibility back to where it belonged.

When he left, the young man was reasonably clear that he had decided neither what kind of job he really wanted to have, nor at what level he should start, because he had never put his training into practice and so consequently did not know its value. What he *did* know, on the other hand, was that he had a coach who was interested in and committed to his job search, but that the search would not be driven by the coach. He also realised that his search, as a result of not really having 'owned' it himself, was vague and undefined. He needed to take the time to go home and do more planning before, on his own initiative, returning for a new coaching session.

Two days later he came back on his own initiative. He asked for interview training, sent in a job application the same day and was offered an interview with a staffing company the following Monday!

FROM SECOND BEST TO LIVING HER DREAM

Two years ago, an assistant nurse at a local council nursing home for older people had her authority to dispense medication removed. Just at the same time, she lost her job and was subsequently signed off sick. Since then, having reluctantly agreed to be assessed as fit to work, she had been applying for other jobs which did not involve any nursing or caring.

However, she kept coming back to her old dream of working in the care of older people because 'they gave her so much back'.

That winter her employment officer met her several times and mentioned her attitude – that she was 'beating around the bush'. It became clear to her that she was only kidding herself, applying for a job in another field, when what she really wanted was to go back into care of the elderly.

Today, she has not yet regained her right to dispense medicines, but she has been able to re-establish her confidence in herself as a person in other nursing homes, and is currently on their lists of temporary relief staff.

NEW WAY OF LOOKING AT HIS SKILLS

A sales assistant in a petrol station was made redundant because it closed down, and he thought the outlook in the small place he lived in was bleak, especially for someone of his background with no qualifications or training. He was focused on trying to obtain some menial job at a local factory.

When his coach heard him relate what he had had responsibility for at the petrol station, it became clear that this man had basically developed the shop's entire range of products all by himself, and had seen to it that the sales had increased. In his own eyes he could not do anything because he just "stood in the shop".

Having taken stock of his skills and competences, it became clear that he had some well-developed sales skills, but that he was totally unaware of it. When he changed his attitude from "I can't do anything and am untrained" to one in which he acknowledged his skills, he got a sales job at a major manufacturing company which had offices in a large town some 100 km away. He was given a company car and was sent on several training courses abroad by his new employer. He could not have imagined this new career when he was made redundant and he thanked his lucky stars for being laid off from his previous job.

VICTIM OF CIRCUMSTANCES TAKES RESPONSIBILITY FOR THE REAL BARRIERS

A group of people with special needs asked their employment officer for coaching. Among them was a very enthusiastic man who dreamed of supporting young gaming addicts to break the habit. He could also imagine himself working with other at-risk people in a residential setting or such like. However, the man was hampered by the care of his young son. When he applied for jobs, he always fell down due to the fact that he could not work nights and weekends. His job search had become deadlocked because of incompatible aims.

Through coaching he became aware of his unproductive attitude, that it was "impossible to get a job because circumstances were the way they were". He realized that he had to change his attitude if he wanted to get a job. When he was able to lower his expectations, his situation changed completely. With the help of New Start funding from the Job Centre, a local golf club employed him as a golf course keeper.

This was able to happen only because he took responsibility for his unrealistic goals and instead set new short-term goals, which would work for him until such time as he was able to leave his son unsupervised and revert to his original plan. And the man's special need? This never actually came up.

FROM DEPENDENT TO INDEPENDENT

An Iraqi agronomist came every week wanting help with everything from training courses to work experience opportunities. He also believed that his coach in their role as employment officer would be able to give him a job.

When his employment officer pointed out that his attitude was that he 'needed help' and showed he was not taking personal responsibility, things started to change.

The man decided to apply for a job in the manufacturing industry, because he felt that he would be unable to get a job as an agronomist without extensive retraining, something he neither wanted to do nor had the time for. In fact, he did not really feel like working as an agronomist either.

So the employment officer coached him in how to present himself as a resource to employers, and how to be convincing about his career change.

This jobseeker is very happy nowadays. Before, he was always being given a lot of advice and tips by the employment office on how to get a job as an agronomist, something he deep down did not want to work as.

FROM FOCUSING ON BARRIERS TO FOCUSING ON STRENGTHS

A woman who was a part-time worker and was on sickness benefit wanted to work as a shop assistant. She had been out of work for a long time, and whenever the employment officer asked her about her future, she explained that she was afraid that an employer would not understand that she did not want a full-time job.

This worry made her only talk about her health issues, and not about what she would be able to offer to a retail business. The coach asked her:

"When you are working in a shop, are you good at what you do?"

"Yes, of course I am," she said, "I'm very good."

"What a pity that you don't let the world know that. At the moment you only talk about what you can't do."

'Clink' – the penny dropped. A week later, on her own initiative she returned to the Job Centre and said that she needed help to write a new application form, because the one she had only focused on her health issues.

HIS DREAM WAS WITHIN REACH

A 30-year-old was working as an Administrative Officer in a central government body, but deep down he dreamed about starting work as a salesman and consultant in the family heating pump business. However, he saw this as a dream with no real basis in reality. His coach observed that his unproductive attitude was that he did not want to take risks but could only take action if he felt he had a guarantee of success. When the man saw how much this pattern of behaviour held him back, he made up his mind that he had what it takes to succeed as a salesman. He started getting experience by work-shadowing another sales rep and got to learn about the salesman role, the products and the technical solutions. Sometime later he resigned as Administrative Officer and started working as a sales rep in his family's business, even though he went onto an uncertain commission-based income.

'SAFE' SEARCHING IS NOT ALWAYS SUCCESSFUL

A woman in her 40s worked in an HR department. Because of cutbacks she was made redundant. She applied for a number of different jobs, was interviewed for all of them, but did not get any. In coaching she received the feedback that she had abandoned her "I want" attitude, as she had only applied for the kind of jobs that she believed she would be able to get based on her qualifications, but which she in fact did not really want at all. When she instead started to think about what she really wanted, she very quickly got her 'must have' job, namely working with skills development.

SECTION 8
COACHING GROUPS

LAYING THE GROUNDWORK FOR COACHING IN GROUPS

In this section, I describe what you should take into consideration when you have a group of jobseekers to coach.

For best possible results you should of course, as group coach, adopt a coaching 'way of being'. Exactly as we went through on the individual coaching level, it involves integrating the five coaching attitudes. The five attitudes in this case are:

- Relating to the group as a group of capable individuals.

- Responsibility – each member of the group is responsible for their own job search.

- Clarifying and focusing instead of giving the group solutions.

- Accepting things as they are – the starting-point in the group is the current situation as it really is and your job is to accept this.

- Not having your own agenda – the work of the group will build on the participants' own agenda (to find a job).

Very many government jobseeking programmes and courses have excellent course material which focuses on how to get a job. The material may be brilliant, but if your group has 'course fatigue' and lack of motivation, the course material simply will not help them.

When you start working with a new group, coaching creates good groundwork for the conditions that have to exist in order to be able to start working with the course material. If you want to use coaching here, do not start using the materials until the solid groundwork has been laid for the participants' cooperation and participation.

Of vital importance to success is the platform you create for all your work together. The platform in its turn depends on how the group participates and how they relate to the activities in the programme. This groundwork means that participants get the opportunity to shift their attitudes and change their outlooks, which will create the conditions for them to independently take charge of their job searches, and for you to coach them.

The following is how an unproductive attitude from a group participant may sound:

> "I'll have to see if there's anything in this for me. I doubt if it can help. But I'll join in. I haven't got anything better to do, have I? I doubt if this is any better than the previous programme I was in."

These are examples of productive attitudes from participants in a group:

> "It offers a support structure which I can use to succeed in my job search."
>
> "I'll get a job myself – but I have a coach for support!"

In order to get the group to adopt a more productive attitude, you as programme leader need to give the participants a chance to choose their attitude to and position on the following points:

- their relationship to the activities and groundrules for the group
- mistrust and scepticism
- what's in it for me?
- what do I need a coach for?
- choosing to participate
- going from consumer to producer
- who's responsible for getting the job?
- am I prepared to consider it possible to get a job?
- will we change the circumstances or get a job?
- the communication contract.

I will go through all these points below, with concrete suggestions on what you need to talk about with the group and what the results/outcomes should be. Prepare yourself by being totally focused on the mood/atmosphere in the room. Listen even before you start coaching. If, for example, the group have a coffee together beforehand, try to judge the mood there.

WHAT YOU NEED TO TALK ABOUT

RELATIONSHIP TO THE ACTIVITIES AND GROUNDRULES FOR THE GROUP

What mood are the participants in? There is a really big risk that they will feel they have been 'sent there' and did not have any choice. They may have resigned themselves regarding the possibilities of getting work. It can also be that they lack confidence in, and are sceptical towards, the organisation which set up the scheme.

All this has to be laid out on the table by asking the group to openly and honestly say what they think about being there. I recommend that you write down in key words what your participants say. All you do here is reflect or 'parrot' what they say. When the exercise is complete, summarize what they have said.

The aim is that the participants get to say everything they are sitting thinking and that they are fully heard, so that the atmosphere in the group can change.

When you have given a summary, you have to map out the themes that have emerged, structure them and present them. Some of the themes may be found in the points below.

MISTRUST AND SCEPTICISM

If a theme in the group is lack of confidence or scepticism, you need to deal with this. You do that by giving the participants the opportunity to air their scepticism and define it. Your work is to listen and summarise so that they feel heard and are given the chance to choose to invest new trust in it or not.

Example:

Coach: So up until now you haven't felt you've had good support from us?

Participant 1: That's right. You're only interested in your own paperwork and making sure the boxes are ticked.

Participant 2: I haven't been able to meet my keyworker for six months.

Coach: I'm really sorry that it hasn't worked out for you. I can see why you feel unhappy.

Once everything has been aired, it is about you, as coach and representative of the organisation, to ask for a second chance.

Example:

Coach: I totally understand that your confidence in me/us is really low at the moment, and that you are sceptical about this programme. The purpose of this exercise is to increase your chances on the job market, and I know it can do that. But it won't work if you don't have any confidence in me/us or the activities. At the same time, I totally respect that you feel at your wits' end and find it hard to trust us. My question to you is: can you give me/us a second chance?

Participant: Well, maybe, but what's the difference between this scheme and the previous ones?

Coach: What is it about the other programmes that didn't work for you?

Participant: They didn't lead anywhere!

Coach: Maybe I can tell you what makes this programme offer a better chance of succeeding, and then you can decide whether you want to give it a chance?

All Participants: Yes, do that.

Coach: Are you prepared to consider that this programme might work?

All Participants: OK, we're listening.

Never try to talk about the value of the programme with the participants until you have their word that they want to consider that there might be something of value in it for them, i.e. until there is an interest in listening. If your participants are crossing their

> **Never try to talk about the value of the programme until they are interested in listening!**

arms, looking sceptical, do not get into trying to explain the value of the programme. You have to deal with the scepticism first, and you do that by bringing it up and talking about it.

WHAT'S IN IT FOR ME?

Like all who have something to offer, the basic position is that you yourself are able to accept whether the participants think, or do not think, it will work. In other words, you have to be able to handle a "no, thank you". The paradox in this is that the more freely you can accept a "no", the more you will get "yes".

You yourself must also fully and freely give your backing to the programme and to the conviction that it is of real importance to the participants. If you are not 100% convinced yourself, you will never be able to convince anyone else. So check the basics first – the responsibility lies with you. Can you handle a "no, thanks"? Are you 100% behind the claim that the programme will give the participants a result, i.e. a job?

When I am selling jobseeking activities to groups, I make sure I take up the following points:

Coach: This programme can increase your chances in the job market. It'll do that for two reasons:

The first reason is that we start from the basic assumption that you will be doing all the work, that you will be managing the job search. It's about you getting the job you want, achieving an outcome that is both long-term and sustainable, and nobody else can do this for you. If you opt to participate in this scheme, you are responsible for, and must manage, your own job search.

The second reason that this programme can increase your chances on the job market is that you have a skilled coach as a resource. I am able to see what it is about you that is preventing you from getting a job. And my task, as your coach, is to give you frank and honest feedback about what is standing in your way. It may be that you're not active enough, but it can also be the way you are doing things (as happens to all of us), for example that you talk too much, don't listen enough, or aren't completely convinced that you have something to offer. Our meetings will get right to the heart of what is preventing you from getting a job. I won't coach you if you don't want me to. Each and every one of you in this group must commission me as their coach. It's your decision if you want to be coached. But this programme consists of personal coaching.

These are the two main reasons why it can be said that this programme will significantly improve your chances of getting a job. Now, what questions do you have?

The point is that the participants understand what they can get out of joining in the activities, and that they actively choose to take part.

WHAT DO I NEED A COACH FOR?

The purpose of using a coach is that *you will get a job faster*. You need to communicate this to the group in an instructive way. It may sound like this:

Coach: If you want to increase your chances of getting a job you want, or need to get a job quickly, you should consider having a coach. A coach's most important task is to spot the unproductive attitudes in the jobseeker – things that the jobseeker themselves are blind to or don't think are essential. Then you can choose to change your approach.

Let us say that a jobseeker feels that they do not have anything to offer an employer. This is an unproductive attitude that is going to hold them back from getting a job. I take it up directly with the person when I am coaching:

Coach: If you yourself don't believe that you have anything to offer, then nobody else will be able to see the point of you. The critical factor is that you can value what you have to offer. How should we tackle this?

Sometimes it is hard work having a coach, who will certainly be saying things that the jobseeker does not want to hear. But one thing is certain: if a person listens to their coach, they will get a result, and that is what you need to communicate to each and every member of the group before the coaching starts.

Coach: If you are really anxious to get a job as soon as possible, then it is a really smart move to have a coach.

That the participants realise the value of having a coach is crucial if they are to benefit from their coaching.

CHOOSING TO PARTICIPATE

It is unfortunate that so many participants in this kind of programme feel that it is obligatory that they attend, that they have no other choice but to take part. In the worst case scenario they are there as a 'victim' or under protest, which can generate a number of unproductive attitudes, such as:

> "They forced me to come here, but there's no way they can force me into anything else."

The fact that many participants are compelled to come on a programme is a very unhelpful starting-point. You can improve the conditions for having a productive attitude by introducing the programme at an introductory meeting, where you 'sell' the programme and let those who are there voluntarily choose to participate or not.

But if you are standing there in front of a group and know that the starting-point is the worst possible, you can deal with it in the following way:

Coach: If I were to ask you to choose to participate in this programme of your own free will, what would you say?

Participant: But you know we have to be here, we don't have a choice ...

Coach: Yes, I know you feel forced into it ...

Participant: What do you mean? We *were* forced into it!

Coach: OK, you *were* forced into it. What I know about participants who join a programme because they are forced to is that they don't get anything from it. I know you want to get you a job, and I want that too. But I also know that you're not going to get a job if you are on the programme because you have to be. To achieve an outcome, you have to choose to participate voluntarily. So I'm going to ask you to do an impossible thing. Although you don't have a choice, I'm asking you to *choose* to participate!

(This is where you get a concrete verbal agreement from each person in the group, one by one.)

Coach: Do you choose to participate voluntarily?

Participant: Yes.
(etc.)

If anyone is doubtful, ask if there is anything they need in order to be able to choose to take part, anything they need to say or need to know. It is perfectly alright if they do not say "yes", but then they cannot be part of the programme.

GOING FROM CONSUMER TO ACTIVIST

The next theme in laying the groundwork is that participants need to see the programme as their own job hunting 'project', a place where their respective job searches can live and develop. The alternative is to sit on a course and be a consumer – a bit like going to the cinema. But this is not a course or a training exercise. It is a structure which can support all their 'projects'. The coach does the coaching and the participants support each other.

Coach: So, I don't want you to participate as if you're at the cinema and I'm the movie. I want you to participate as if this is the workplace setting for your own projects. We will be discussing things to do with job hunting and the job market. And the more you direct your own project and ask for what you need, the more useful it will be for yourself.

So, what is required from you as participants? Well, that you:

- participate voluntarily
- have a concrete aim
- are open to coaching and feedback
- are ready for straight talking
- see yourself as responsible for your own job search and act accordingly
- stick to the groundrules.

In addition, it helps to start your sessions by asking:

Coach: How do you want to use me today?

Coach: What is the most pressing thing for us to discuss right now (in relation to where you are with your job search)?

WHO IS RESPONSIBLE FOR GETTING THE JOB?

A precondition for getting a job is that the participants see it as their responsibility and nobody else's. Part of the groundwork is to sort out at this stage the notion of where the responsibility lies:

Coach: I'd like to take a closer look at the question of who's going to get a job for you. Who do you think will get you a job?

Lead the discussion and let all views be expressed, while at the same time firmly sticking to the position that "nobody can get you a job except you yourself". A common theme is the illusion that somebody else should fix up the work.

Coach: That somebody else is going to get a job for us is an illusion which we all share, though we know that this is not really how it works.

(At this point the participants easily take up a defensive stance:)

Participant: So, you don't feel we are taking responsibility?

Coach: I don't have any thoughts about what you take responsibility for at this point. What I'm saying is that the more responsibility you take for you own job search, the faster you will get results.

When this subject has been exhausted, most usually agree that it is each individual's own personal responsibility to find work. Make a verbal agreement with the participants at this point:

Coach: Can we agree that in this group each person takes responsibility for ensuring that they get a job, with support and encouragement from me and the group?

(If someone is doubtful, ask coaching questions:)

Coach: So, how do you want to see this working? How will you set about getting a job, if you don't want to see yourself taking responsibility for it?

(Of course, pose your questions politely and with respect and empathy, without being confrontative.)

CAN I CONSIDER IT POSSIBLE?

As I mentioned in the section on individual coaching, a crucial step is to consider that it is possible to actually get a job. In group coaching you discuss this as a group. Use your white board and draw the two circles:

Impossible   *Consider it possible*

Coach: The most decisive factor in how your job search will go is how you view the likelihood of getting a result. If you're doubtful about getting a job, you won't get a job. If you consider that there is one job out there for you, you have dramatically increased the possibilities in your job search.

In the "circle of impossibilities", it's comfortable and risk free; in the "circle of possibilities" things are risky and uncertain. In the circle of impossibilities you don't need to take responsibility, you can just sit back and complain in comfort. In the circle of possibilities, you have to take responsibility for making the opportunities a reality.

That's why we humans easily end up in the circle of impossibilities. The tiresome thing about that is that there are no jobs to be had there. None.

It's from the circle of possibilities that you need to start when you are directing your own job hunt. If you are driving it from the circle of impossibilities, you might as well save your energy and do nothing. It just isn't going to deliver a result.

So I'm going to ask you all to consider the possibility that there actually is *one single* job for you.

(Go round the group and ask each person individually to answer the question of whether they consider it possible that there is one job for them. If anyone doubts this, coach them as follows:)

Coach: What is it that makes you doubtful? How would you like to take things forward? Do you want to stay in the circle of impossibilities? How do you then plan to take part in this programme? Is it possible to do that?

(Let the person take responsibility for their choice. Accept the person's choice, but be clear that the programme is not for them.)

Until the participants think it is possible to get a job, there is no point in coaching them to find one.

WILL WE CHANGE THE CIRCUMSTANCES OR GET A JOB?

Some groups have a tendency to start talking about all the circumstances that are wrong: the situation in the job market is bad; they live in the wrong area; the wrong government is in power; Job Centres are useless; there are no jobs around etc. If the group were allowed to discuss over and over again everything that should be different, nothing would be achieved.

For the meetings with the group to be constructive, you have to ask the group members how they want to use their time.

Coach: Are you going to change the world, or are you going to get a job? If you want to change the world, I won't agree to be your coach.

Participants quickly realise this. Make an agreement with them all that they dedicate themselves to finding a job (in the world as it is, with all its deficiencies), and that you want them to give you the mandate to point out if they are slipping back into being "world reformers", so that they get back on track.

THE COMMUNICATION CONTRACT

In order to stop people talking rubbish and undermining the discussions, you may make an agreement with the participants that if they have complaints about you, or problems with the activities, they will raise them with you and nobody else. Here is an example of a groundrule:

Coach: If you have a problem with someone or something, take it up with the person concerned and sort it out between yourselves. If you have views about the organisation of the programme, or me as course leader, come and talk to me about it.

TRAPS WHEN COACHING GROUPS

The most common trap of all when you stand in front of a group is that you start to spout theory. We are all products of a school system, which means that we automatically assume the classroom roles of teacher and student. When this happens, there is great risk of people merely sitting back and soaking it in, with a worse outcome as a result.

As far as possible, set up the room not as a classroom but rather as a workplace. And be careful that you don't fall into the role of 'producer'. Here are some other traps:

- You start arguing about what the group is saying. This is totally inappropriate. Let them have their experiences without challenging; your job is to listen.

- You rush through this part because it is uncomfortable or 'unnecessary'. You think "we must get down to the real work".

- The participants become impatient because the situation feels uncomfortable. Be firm that this stage is important.

- You are not listening with your full attention.

CONCLUDING WORDS ABOUT GROUP COACHING

When you have laid the groundwork with the help of the different steps I have described above, and ensured the group's commitment, then you have already done more than half of the coaching task, maybe more. The more you set unproductive attitudes loose (something we normally avoid because we are unable to control it) the more quickly you will arrive in the productive atmosphere on the other side.

Look to yourself. It is you who need to change your attitude from "this is not how it should be" to "this is how it is right now". *Use* the group's whingeing, and stop thinking in terms of "we must get this over and done with". Nothing is more important than what is happening here and now, you gain nothing from rushing on to something else. The atmosphere is how it is, and is not about right or wrong. It is just a question of how to relate to it. For you, it is all about 'accepting the situation', setting aside your own agenda and not thinking "this is hard work, I don't want this".

> **Nothing is more important than what is happening here and now!**

It is in the here and now that results are created, not later, even if we believe that it is the management of the project and 'being active' that are most important. This is not how it works. As this book shows, it is the *attitude to what is done* that determines the outcome.

Now it is about starting to work. But keep an eye on the group atmosphere and mood throughout. And bear in mind that you now have a number of groundrules that you can fall back on. Some examples:

Coach: Now I feel that you are not focusing on the possibilities any more. What happened?

Coach: I hear gossip about you being unhappy. What happened to our communication contract? What is it you haven't said to me?

Coach: Now I feel you are putting the responsibility on me again. Who is responsible for getting you a job?

The important thing for the ongoing work is that you coach the group exactly as you would coach an individual. Give the responsibility back to the group whenever it 'drifts over' to you.

At this stage, you can start using the course material or course content that you had planned to use. But continue to bear in mind not to let the material take over, otherwise it is easy for the participants to start becoming 'consumers' and lose focus on their respective job searches and aims. Let the course material be of secondary importance and support the participants from the position they are in.

SECTION 9
TRAINING SUPPORT

SUPPORT TO HELP YOU GET STARTED

Now that you have read the book, you have hopefully acquired a number of new approaches, but still only in theory. This is in principle pointless until you have started applying these approaches through training. To begin training is essential in order to achieve all that can be achieved. Below is some help to get started on your training.

COMMITMENT

You will be coaching many different individuals in making a commitment to the future they want to bring about and then standing fast to that commitment regardless of circumstances. That is how we all achieve our goals.

If you want to become a skilled coach, you must do the same thing as the people you are coaching, make a commitment that is personal to you and your training as a coach. There is no other way.

As with all training, there is always an inbuilt resistance to getting started. Make sure you are prepared to fight that resistance.

REMINDERS

Training and development is something which, unhelpfully, is constantly being deprioritised in favour of seemingly more 'important' tasks. Don't allow your training to be pushed down the priority list if you are serious about your ambitions. One tip is to set up different reminders about your training, for example in the form of promises to others, a message on your computer/mobile phone or setting aside time in your calendar.

PART OF YOUR DAILY LIFE

There are endless opportunities for you to practise your coaching *attitude* outside of the workplace, for example in your relationship with your children and their friends, when your friends are in distress, or in work with clubs and societies.

Above all, most coaches need to practise giving open and honest feedback. I am sure you can think straightaway of ten situations where you can practise this in your daily life.

Just remember that under no circumstances do you have the right to start coaching a person who has not explicitly asked for it. If you do, you will only come up against irritation and disapproval from people around you. On the other hand, you are free to adopt a coaching *attitude* in any situation.

TRAPS ARE THE KEY TO YOUR FUTURE SKILLS

Make sure you take every opportunity to fall into as many traps as possible. Riders are usually told that the more often they fall off the horse, the faster they become good riders. It is the same with coaching. It is taking lots of risks in your dialogues that will develop your skills fastest. See also the paragraph below about traps in the context of starting-points.

PLAN YOUR TRAINING

Organise your ongoing training by setting aside 30 minutes each week to meet up with your coaching colleagues to take part in a role play. One person role-plays an actual person and another is the coach. Introduce a new routine which involves always using a colleague as a sounding board whenever you have in any way felt 'stuck' in a coaching conversation. Make sure you do it as soon as possible after the coaching session. It need only take 15 minutes. Do not go into another coaching conversation until you have done it! Acquire your own local coaching trainer, by finding someone who is more skilled at coaching than you are and who you can do mini training sessions with.

MAKE SURE YOU GET FEEDBACK

You are blind to your own traps! The biggest barrier to becoming better at the coaching dialogue is to believe you can already coach. Yes, you probably have good dialogues with the people you are supporting, but if you are like most other people, there is enormous potential within you. And the more feedback you open yourself up to, the more you can tap into this potential. That way you have the opportunity to recognise the traps that you were blind to a moment before.

Those who know most are those closest to you: friends, partner and children. These people are a virtual goldmine of information if you can get them to be honest about your communication skills, listening skills and the ability to be 'present'.

CONFRONT TRAPS

If you have been coaching for a good while and think you are starting to be quite accomplished, but still want to reach a higher level, the route there is to go back to working on your most common development points. So which of the five attitudes is your underdeveloped skill, the trap you fall into whenever you fall into a trap? Choose just *one* and confront yourself, using the guide below.

	Traps	Confronting the traps	Exercises
Relating to people's potential	I have difficulty seeing the jobseeker as competent. I judge people as incapable, instead of considering that perhaps they are operating in adverse circumstances.	Confront your own arrogance towards others. Who gave you the right to decide what the jobseeker can or can't do? Reflect on the fact that strength and competence have different modes of expression.	Make a list of 3 people who you don't have confidence in and describe each one in terms of their abilities.
Whose responsibility?	I don't dare risk getting a negative result, so I compensate for the incapability of others by taking on too much responsibility for them and their job searches. I tell them what to do instead of releasing their own power.	Where in your own life do you take on responsibilities which are not yours? How would your reality look if you stopped taking responsibility for others? What does it cost you to take on other people's responsibilities? What stops you from letting go of responsibilities which are not yours?	Be excessively irresponsible! Let a situation break down by refusing to take responsibility. Be concrete about where and how you will do this.
Clarifying and focusing	I like my own ideas and solutions, so encourage a passive mood when the jobseeker comes to me for tips and ideas, or is inspired by my ideas. I have an ambition to be able to accept the suggestions of others, but am actually focused on my own ideas and don't hear what they are saying.	Confront yourself with this: who wants to know what you think? What are your views really worth? You are robbing jobseekers of their creativity and desired outcomes. You make them dependent on your ideas and solutions and, in the long run, on you. You are not interested in others. You talk too much!	Listen to people's ideas (i.e. be quiet!). Ask "What do you think...?" 20 times a week. Be quiet at a meeting – BE QUIET. Note down what you hear.

	Weaknesses/traps	Feedback	Training tips
Accepting the situation	I think that people 'should be better'. If the jobseekers would only sharpen themselves up a bit and do what they should, everything would come right.	Confront yourself with the fact that you think you have a monopoly on the truth, and if others don't think the same way as you … what then? Identify your own 'way of being'. Confront yourself with the fact that you are actually working against the jobseeker's way of being instead of accepting the situation.	Practise acceptance. Identify 3 things that you do not accept. Your homework is to learn to accept them.
Not having your own agenda	I expect my coaching to lead to a specific outcome.	You can't coach/strengthen/ empower anyone if you don't accept their aims and solutions.	Find opportunities to stop planning ahead and drawing up strategies. Go to your coaching sessions unprepared and ask "What do you want?" Connect with their agenda. Specify their aims.

ALL THE EXERCISES IN THE BOOK

Exercise 1
Read the statements below and notice which ones most strike you. They give important clues as to where the key traps for you lie when it comes to listening. If after reading them you say, "These are all pitfalls for me", then that is a pitfall in itself. The value for you comes in being specific and really being concrete about one or two from the list.

- I don't listen to the end. I jump in and fill in what I think the other person is going to say.
- While I'm listening, I'm also wondering what the other person thinks of me. (I feel like I have to perform.)
- My thoughts often drift to what I see as the most relevant bit of the conversation or the part I associate with most.
- I listen more in order to be able to provide an answer, rather than to understand.
- When the topic of conversation interests me, I wait for the other person to stop talking so that I can say my bit.
- I think in advance about what I want to say next.
- I concentrate so much on appearing interested that I hardly hear a word.
- I lose concentration if the other person talks for too long, or if I'm not interested in the subject.
- I try to listen even when I don't actually have the time.
- I keep thinking about whether what the person is saying seems logical or illogical, right or wrong, true or false.
- I listen most to the spoken words and don't take in the tone of voice, the body language or facial expressions.
- If I get impatient, I interrupt.
- I am easily distracted by things around me.

Once you have picked out your key stumbling-blocks when you are listening, think about which situations usually make you fall into these patterns of not listening. What sorts of people do you tend to listen to least? How do you usually behave in these situations?

Now the work starts to observe on a daily basis when you have ended up in a trap. In other words, be conscious of it and then choose a different way of behaving to your usual one. The more you dare to acknowledge the traps – in other words, the more feedback you accept and the clearer your patterns of behaviour become – the easier it will be for you to be aware of them and change them.

In order to remember to keep being attentive to your way of listening, you could put up reminders to support yourself, for example a note saying "How am I listening?" on the door of your fridge or on your screen saver. If there are others in your workplace who are coaches, ask them continually for feedback. Ask them to tell you when you fall into a trap if you happen to do so at coffee break. Anyone who has previously given you feedback can keep giving you reminders. If you are supporting someone in a coaching conversation, reflect extra carefully upon your listening skills during the session.

Exercise 2

A useful tool is the 'parroting' technique, which involves you repeating back what the other person says, using their own words. Again, if you have children, try this on them – they'll love it!

Example:

Child: I made three paper kites at school today, Dad!

Dad: Oh, so you made three paper kites at school today!

Child: Yes, a blue one, a green one and a pink one. The pink one was the best!

Dad: I see. One blue kite, one green kite, and the best one – the pink one.

Child: Yes, and it was really difficult to cut them out. Anna helped to get the tails right.

Dad: I see. They were difficult to cut out, especially the tails, so Anna helped you.

As a parent you are normally bored to death after the first statement and parroting is a real pain. But believe me, this exercise can have magic results in several ways. Partly you come to discover how unused you are to not putting your own contribution into a conversation, and partly you find that the conversation will develop much more than if you block it with your comments. Try it!

Exercise 3

The following is a variation on the previous exercise. Have a conversation with someone where you only summarise what the other person says, after each time they have spoken. Notice how long it takes the other person to move towards their own solution merely by parroting them. Give this technique a try, and try to disregard how silly or pointless it feels just to repeat what someone else has said. You have to be able to overcome this feeling until it feels quite natural to 'just' repeat.

This is a skill that you will be using often during your coaching – not adding your own input, just bringing something to the surface by repeating it. The important thing is that your contributions are totally neutral and free from your own additions, interpretations and conclusions. In order to achieve this, you need to learn to live with being reduced to the role of a 'parrot'.

Exercise 4

Ask a friend or colleague if you may coach them in some dilemma they have, using only the questions listed above. There is no need to ask the questions in the exact order in which they stand, but restrict yourself only to these.

Pay special attention to what you tend to do *instead of* asking these questions and listening to the answers – it will indicate the traps you tend to fall into.

In order to improve your skills, ask for specific feedback on how you ask your questions during a coaching conversation. Ask the person to be brutally honest so that you can recognise your tendencies and the traps you fall into. This is an important key to improving the quality of your dialogues.

Exercise 5

Try a role play with someone who is skilled at dialogues. Ask for their feedback with a focus just on your questioning. The two central issues that you want to clarify are: "Can I ask questions at all?" and "How good are the questions I ask?"

Rate your questions on the following scale, with 1 representing the poorest response and 4 the best:

1. I only get monosyllabic and useless answers.
2. I get valid answers but I seem to be doing most of the work.
3. I get full and comprehensive answers, and the person opposite me is engaged.
4. The other person is thinking and reflecting, and is clearly working hard on formulating their answers.

Based on the feedback you get from this exercise, you should be able to identify one or more traps in the way you are asking questions. It may be that they are too long and complicated; that you don't wait for an answer; that you are thinking about your next question before you have heard the response to your previous one; that you don't listen to the answer so don't know what to ask next; that you don't really ask questions, you just tell the person what they should do (i.e. you are giving advice); and so on. These are just a few examples, but you may well identify others.

Once you have become aware of the quality of your questioning skills, you can identify what you need to work on.

Exercise 6

Think about a person you are coaching whom you are finding particularly difficult. It can be a person that you get a slightly uneasy feeling about as soon as you see that they have booked in for a session. When you are with this person you always get a premonition that the discussion is not going to lead anywhere. What unproductive attitude or way of being does this person have?

Exercise 7

Pick two TV show presenters that you know. Choose one you like and one you dislike. What attitude or way of being does the person you dislike have?

You are now training yourself to listening to the way of being rather than to comments, statements or actions. You can do this in any situation: on the bus, at home with your family, in front of the TV. What you want to acquire is the ability to be able to specify attitudes and ways of being.

Exercise 8

An efficient way to train is, after a coaching session, to reflect by asking yourself the question: "What unproductive attitude does this person have that is preventing them from achieving their aim?" As you keep on training you will identify several different attitudes, some of which may be: passive, 'single-tracked', compliant, careless, lacking in initiative. Each and every one of these can be specified and defined even more, so that they hit the mark more accurately. Some suggestions:

Passive	uninterested, having a 'let's wait-and-see' attitude, lazy, indifferent, resigned, "dead"
'Single-tracked'	rigid, remote, unreceptive, stubborn, static, fanatical
Compliant	indecisive, vacillating, easily influenced, fickle, turns whichever way the

	wind is blowing, self-sacrificing, biddable
Careless	not hot on details, blasé, gives only 85 percent, cuts corners, unreliable, a fantasist with no handle on reality, slipshod, sloppy
Lacking in initiative	dejected, plays the victim, lazy, spoilt, paralysed, a jellyfish

When you get more specific in this way you notice that the first adjectives are quite neutral and tame. But deep down you are probably thinking rather of the other, more uncensored, words. These blunt adjectives can be extremely valuable to the jobseeker, so teach yourself to be concrete and uncensored. Ask yourself what you really think about the person you are coaching.

Exercise 9

Ask someone to practise coaching with you. Pick the worst attitude or manner that you can think of: aggressive, patronizing, confrontational, scatterbrained etc. Choose an attitude and ask your sparring partner to role-play a person with that attitude. You introduce your coaching session by saying: "How is it going with your job search?" The other person responds, trying to exhibit the difficult attitude or manner.

Your task is to give very clear feedback on this attitude as soon as possible. As soon as you have done that, you can end the exercise. Reflect on how it was for you. Were you impeded from giving your feedback and if so, why? Analyse what was holding you back. What did you do instead of giving feedback – for example, were you waiting for the right moment? Ask your partner for feedback on how straightforward and clear you were.

Exercise 10

If you want to intensify your training even further, look around you at your relationships with others and see if you have cause to raise something? The thing that is casting obstacles in your way as a coach is actually the same fear that makes you have unresolved issues with your nearest and dearest. So the more you challenge your fear, the better coaching skills you acquire. In all likelihood, you will get tangibly better relationships into the bargain. If not, you can assume that there is something about your way of being that is not empowering the other person. If this is the case, go back to the five points in Section 1 on the coaching approach.

SECTION 10
AND FINALLY

RESPONDING TO THE CHALLENGES

I now return to the challenges which I introduced at the beginning of my book. I will respond to the questions only briefly as the idea is that once you have read and digested the book's contents, you will hopefully have your own perspectives on the problems.

HOW DO I MOTIVATE A PERSON WHO HAS GIVEN UP HOPE?

It is not your task as a coach to motivate someone else. When you come up against resignation or lack of motivation, you mirror this with the purpose of letting the person you are coaching take responsibility for their resignation and lack of motivation.

HOW DO I COACH SPOILT YOUNG PEOPLE WHO DON'T WANT TO DO ANYTHING AT ALL?

Firstly, you make sure that you do not become provoked by their spoilt behaviour. Then you can mirror that behaviour or attitude which is holding them back and is not helping them. Give frank and honest feedback without showing agitation. Everyone wants something, it is just that some have difficulty realising exactly what it is they want. This is what coaching is all about. A spoilt young person will not open up until they feel that you are taking their aspirations seriously and treating them with respect.

WHAT DO I DO ABOUT SOMEONE WHO HIDES BEHIND THEIR HEALTH ISSUES, EVEN WHEN THEY HAVE NOT BEEN SIGNED OFF SICK?

First you find out what they really want and the fears that they have which make them no longer want to talk about it. What would their goals be if there were not "ifs" and "buts"? If they think that their actual goals are impossible and unrealistic, challenge them to consider the possibility of giving their real goal a chance, with a skilled coach as partner.

HOW DO I GET PEOPLE OVER 55 TO WANT TO HAVE A JOB?

If the person over 55 really does not want to have a job, there is no remedy for this. It is a fact. However, their unwillingness might be hidden resignation, in which case there may be a "yes" behind their "no" which needs to surface.

WHAT DO YOU DO ABOUT SOMEONE WHO DOESN'T UNDERSTAND THAT THEY ARE TOO CHOOSY?

You give frank and honest feedback on their unproductive attitude. I remember one young man who was sitting waiting for a particular job which might become available within two years. I asked him if he was interested in earning a proper living for himself and his children. He said, "Of course, that's why I'm talking to you." I said, "I am asking because I'm unsure why you're gambling with your chances of earning a living. You've placed all your bets on 'zero', hoping this will come up. The odds are not particularly good at the moment."

HOW DO YOU GET A PERSON TO RELOCATE IN ORDER TO GET A JOB?

You cannot make another person do something they do not want to do. Having an agenda or solution in mind is counterproductive. The person will start working against your plans (with every justification!) and fight for their right to make their own decisions. Imagine if you were treated in this way, with pressure and directives which would limit your freedom of action. The solution is to let the jobseeker take responsibility and answer to the consequences. "How are you going to handle the fact that the job market is slow, when your aim is to get a job by 1 December?"

WHAT DO YOU DO WHEN EVEN YOU THINK A PERSON IS A HOPELESS CASE?

You start by realising that you see the person as hopeless and ask yourself whether you can consider that this person is actually capable. If you can do this, then you can go on coaching them, otherwise not. Then it is a matter of giving them frank and honest feedback. "Do you know what? I just caught myself thinking of you as a totally hopeless case."

COMMON QUESTIONS

Below I answer some questions which are often put to me in my courses and when I am training coaches.

ISN'T THIS A FORM OF THERAPY?

No, it is not. This coaching method focuses on aspects of a person's behaviour and 'ways of being', which has similarities with psychology or therapy. Also, the conversation often becomes unusually personal because you are focusing on attitudes, and many such issues crop up both in the coaching conversation and on the therapist's couch. But there is one important difference: coaching has the 'here and now' as its starting-point. There is an explicit goal, and it is about coaching people through barriers and fears, with a view to the future. Therapy, on the other hand, looks at underlying causes and tries to understand what has happened before. In coaching, you always start from the present. You do not deal with the past at all.

ISN'T COACHING ENORMOUSLY TIME-CONSUMING?

No, on the contrary, it saves a lot of time. But it requires that you train yourself up to be really proficient, especially when it comes to listening for unproductive attitudes. This is difficult at first.

HOW LONG DOES IT TAKE TO TRAIN TO BE A JOBSEEKER COACH?

It is not really a matter of time, but depends on how brave you are – in other words, the extent to which you are prepared to 'dive in' during the conversation. Six months of continuous training, which includes conversations where you get the chance of feedback, will take you far.

SOME UNCOMFORTABLE TRUTHS ABOUT JOBSEEKER COACHING

Lastly, some words which can be tough to hear but are worth considering nevertheless:

Many jobseeker coaches know exactly why an employer does not employ a person but shy away from giving feedback on this. The excuse they give for avoiding giving feedback is that the jobseeker may become upset, hurt, disappointed or maybe even have a breakdown, when in actual fact frank and honest feedback is their only chance of getting work.

Many jobseeker coaches work exclusively advising others, instead of drawing out people's own abilities.

Many coaches regard jobseekers as helpless and incapable, and start to unconsciously relate to them in this way. This is a huge barrier to the effectiveness of jobseeker coaching.

Jobseeker coaching which is not performed properly is counterproductive: in other words, it will make the jobseeker even more passive than was the case before the coaching began.

Many jobseeker coaches are good at having a dialogue with jobseekers, but what is often missing is the ability to conduct a dialogue that really draws out the other's inherent potential. Yet that is what leads to results!

Many jobseeker coaches also have an official government function, and when that becomes mixed up with coaching, the coaching becomes ineffective.

Many jobseeker coaches let the jobseeker use substandard job application documents when they apply for jobs.

CONCLUDING WORDS

I would like people to be treated really kindly and offered support whenever they find themselves in a difficult situation – a kind of support that makes them want to come back, and be able to achieve what they want. This is one reason that this book came about. I know that my coaching method works in practice and is useful to jobseeker coaches – I have vast proof of this. And I would like to see it used more and become more widespread.

What I hope is also clear from the book is that this method, if used consistently, does not only lead to minor improvements, but can lead to major tangible results of a kind that all parties involved want to see: increased employment, shorter periods of unemployment and, for groups who have been outside the job market, to ability to re-enter it through their own efforts.

Most of all, I have encountered enthusiasm from jobseeker coaches, especially from those in the profession who have a genuine interest in people and a strong desire to support others. For them, what I have to share has complemented their already well-developed coaching ability and has given them the reassurance both that they are working in the right way and that the method is extremely useful, constantly leading to good results in their work to support jobseekers.

However, I do not want to conceal the fact that there is resistance to this approach, objections that people are not really capable. To see certain people as helpless individuals who are too weak to take personal responsibility is a cherished notion which pervades large parts of our public support services. It is usually readily accompanied by the view that seeing people as competent is an expression of elitist thinking – "looking after number one", "to hell with others", cold-hearted cynicism. Every time I end up in such a discussion and do not succeed in getting my message across that the whole method is built on respect, empathy and love for others, I am disappointed, depressed and a bit despairing of the current situation. Whenever government employees adopt an attitude of knowing better than the individual themselves what is best for them, I feel afraid and wonder where we are going as a society.

What I prefer to listen to and rely on, however, is the great response I have had from out there in the field, both from jobseeker coaches working in different organisations, as well as from jobseekers themselves. It is what they tell me about the amazing outcomes and breakthroughs in people's lives that makes me want to go on sharing my experiences and skills, and train others in really effective jobseeker coaching.

ACKNOWLEDGEMENTS

Thank you first and foremost to my close colleague Carl Erik Herlitz, who constantly furnishes me with improvements and without whose input this book would never have come into being. Some of my co-workers and fellow jobseeker coaches, Lotta Borgsten, Marina Marklund and Pi-Charlotte Strindberg, read my manuscript and brought clarity and wisdom. Lotta Höijer and Sylvia Wallgren have for many years been robust and faithful supporters in the development of our web tools and in disseminating the coaching method.

Employment officer Ulf Lindskog has assisted by providing examples, facts and the invaluable perspective of a government official. My friend Alexandra Simpson has done a great job of capturing my way of writing and translating it into English.

A whole host of other people have questioned, reminded, encouraged, supported and coached me, which has contributed to the book's existence. Thanks to you all!

Karin Tenelius